Songs of Jamaica

Songs of Jamaica

Claude McKay

MINT EDITIONS

Songs of Jamaica was first published in 1912.

This edition published by Mint Editions 2021.

ISBN 9781513299358 | E-ISBN 9781513224053

Published by Mint Editions®

MINT
EDITIONS

minteditionbooks.com

Publishing Director: Jennifer Newens
Design & Production: Rachel Lopez Metzger
Project Manager: Micaela Clark
Typesetting: Westchester Publishing Services

To His Excellency
Sir Sydney Olivier, K.C.M.G,
Governor of Jamaica
Who
By His Sympathy With the Black Race
Has Won
The Love and Admiration of All Jamaicans,
This Volume is
By Permission
Respectfully Dedicated

Contents

Preface to "Songs of Jamaica"

What Italian is to Latin, that in regard to English is the negro variant thereof. It shortens, softens, rejects the harder sounds alike of consonants and vowels; I might almost say, refines. In its soft tones we have an expression of the languorous sweetness of the South: it is a feminine version of masculine English; pre-eminently a language of love, as all will feel who, setting prejudice aside, will allow the charmingly naïve love-songs of this volume to make their due impression upon them. But this can only happen when the verses are read aloud, and those unacquainted with the Jamaican tongue may therefore welcome a few hints as to pronunciation.

As a broad general direction, let it be observed that the vowels have rather the continental than the English sounds, while in the matter of the consonants the variation from English is of the nature of a pretty lisp. The exact values of the vowels cannot, of course, be described, but they approximate on the whole more to those of Italy and France than to those of England. One sound, that of *aw*, is entirely rejected, and ah is substituted for it. Thus *bawl*, *law*, *call*, *daughter*, etc., become *bahl*, *lah*, *cahl*, *dahter*, etc.

In the word *whe'*, which sometimes means where and sometimes which, the *e* has the same sound as in the word *met*. *Deh* is similarly pronounced, and the *e* is quite a short one, the *h* being added merely to distinguish *deh* from *de* (the). This short *e* often takes the place of the close English *a*, as in *tek* (take), *mek* (make).

My is almost invariably pronounced with a short *y*, and, to remind the reader of this, it is constantly spelt *me*. *Fe*—generally meaning *to*, but sometimes *for*—matches this short *my* exactly. In *caan'* (can't) the *a* is doubled in order to ensure the pronunciation *cahn*.

It is difficult to convey the exact value of *do'n* (down), *groun'* (ground). There is a faint trace of *ng* at the end of these words, and they rhyme to tongue pronounced very shortly and with a dumber vowel sound.

Vowels are sometimes changed out of mere caprice, as it seems. Thus we have *ef* for *if*, *trimble* for *tremble*, *anedder* for *anudder* (another), *stimulent* for *stimulant*, *a*—pronounced short—for *I*, *sperit* for *spirit*.

In *ya*, originally meaning *d'you hear*—but now thrown in just to fill up, like the *don't you know* of certain talkers—the *a* is a short *ah*.

We come now to the consonants. Bearing in mind what was said above of the pretty lisp, let the *d* so often—generally, we may say—substituted for *th*, be of the very softest, as it were a *th* turning towards *d*, or to put it in another way, a lazily pronounced *th*. The negro has no difficulty whatever in pronouncing it clearly: it is merely that he does not, as a rule, take the trouble to do so. In these poems *the*, *they*, *there*, with, etc., are not always written *de*, *dey*, *dere*, *wid*, etc.; and the reader is at liberty to turn any soft *th* into *d*, and any *d* into soft *th*. And here let me remark, in passing, that in one breath the black man will pronounce a word in his own way, and in the next will articulate it as purely as the most refined Englishman. Where the substitution of *d* makes the word unrecognisable, as in *moder* (mother), *oders* (others), the spelling *mudder*, *udders* is resorted to; and for fear of confusion with well-known words, though, those are always written thus, although generally pronounced, *dough*, *dose*.

As *d* supplants the soft *th*, so does a simple *t* supplant the hard one; as in *t'ing*, *not'ing* (or *nuttin'* ,—for the *g* in words of two or more syllables is very commonly left out), *t'ink*, *tick*, *t'rough*, *met'od*, *wutless* (worthless).

V tends to pass into *b*, as in *lub* (love), *hab*, *lib*, *ebery*, *neber*, *cultibation*. *Vex*, though so written for the most part, is pronounced either with a decided *b* or with some compromise between that and *v*.

Of elisions, the commonest is that of the initial *s* when followed by another consonant. Thus *start*, *spread*, *stop*, *scrape*, *spoil*, *sting*, *skin*, etc., become *'tart*, *'pread*, *'top*, *'crape*, *'poil*, *''ting*, *'kin*, etc.

Final *d's* are often dropped, as in *lan'*, *t'ousan'*, *please'* (pleased) and other past participles, *min'*, *chil'*—in these let care be taken to keep the long sound of the *i'*—*wul'* (world), *wud* (word), *en'*.

Final *t's* also; as in *breas'*, *cas'*, *'gains'* (against), *i'* (it), *las'*, *wha'*, *wus'* (worst), *tas'e* (taste). Present participles, *passin'*, *brukin'* (breaking), *outpourin'*, etc., lose their *g's*; and final *k's* sometimes disappear, as in *tas'*. *R's*, too, as in *you'* for *your*, *mo'* for *more*, *befo'* or simply *'fo'* for *before*: and they are even thrown out from the middle of words, as in *wuk* (work), *tu'n* (turn), *wud* (word). *Will* occasionally loses its *l's* and becomes *wi'*.

Initial vowels have also a habit of vanishing: as in *'bout* (about), *'long* (along), *'way* (away), *nuff* (enough), *'pon* (upon); but the elision of these and of longer first syllables is sometimes made up by tacking something to the end, and for about, without, because we get *'bouten*, *'douten*, *'causen*.

On the construction of the language it is unnecessary to dwell, for it is fully explained in the notes, and the reader will soon master the mysteries of *be'n* with its various significations, *is, was, were, have been, had been, did* (as sign of the past tense); of *deh*, which may be either an adverb (there) or an auxiliary verb as in me deh beg (I am begging); of *dem* tacked close to its noun, to show it is plural; of tenses apparently past which are present, and apparently present which are past: for the unravelling of all which the needful help has, it is hoped, been supplied by the notes aforesaid.

Readers of this volume will be interested to know that they here have the thoughts and feelings of a Jamaican peasant of pure black blood. The young poet, aged twenty-two, spent his early years in the depths of the country, and though he has now moved to the more populous neighbourhood of Kingston, his heart remains in his Clarendon hills. He began life as a wheelwright, but the trade was not to his mind, and he left it and enlisted in the Constabulary.

WALTER JEKYLL

Quashie to Buccra[1]

You tas'e[2] petater[3] an' you say it sweet,
But you no[4] know how hard we wuk[5] fe it;
You want a basketful fe quattiewut[6],
'Cause you no know how 'tiff de bush fe cut[7].

De cowitch[8] under which we hab fe 'toop,
De shamar[9] lyin' t'ick like pumpkin soup,
Is killin' somet'ing[10] for a naygur man;
Much less[11] de cutlass workin' in we han'.

De sun hot like when fire ketch a[12] town;
Shade-tree look temptin', yet we caan' lie down,
Aldough we wouldn' eben ef we could,
Causen we job must finish soon an' good.[13]

De bush cut done, de bank dem we deh dig[14],
But dem caan' 'tan' sake o' we naybor pig;
For so we moul' it up he root it do'n[15],
An' we caan' 'peak sake o' we naybor tongue[16].

---

1. The buccra (white man) looking over the hedge at the Black man's field, is addressed by the latter as follows.
2. Taste.
3. Sweet potato (*Ipomaa Batatas*.)
4. Don't.
5. Work.
6. Quattiworth: quattie, a quarter of sixpence.
7. Because you don't know how stuff the bush is to cut, *i.e.*, what hard work it is to fell the trees and clear the land.
8. *Mucuna pruriens*.
9. Shamebush, the prickly sensitive plant (*Mimosa Pudica*.)
10. Terrible stuff.
11. More.
12. In.
13. Because our job must be quickly and thoroughly done.
14. The clearing of the land done, we dig the banks—kind of terraces on the steep hill side—but owing to our neighbour's pig they cannot stand. "Bank dem" = banks. This intrsutive "dem" must be tacked closely to the preceding word. It occurs again below—"row dem."
15. For no ssoner do we mould it up, than he (the pig) roots it (the bank) down. "Down" is pronounced very short, and is a good rhyme to "tongue."
16. And we cannot complain, for this would "bring confusion," *i.e.*, cause a row.

Aldough de vine is little, it can bear;
It wantin' not'in' but a little care:
You see petater tear up groun', you run,[17]
You laughin', sir, you must be t'ink a fun.[18]

De fie!' pretty? It couldn't less 'an dat[19],
We wuk de bes',[20] an' den de lan' is fat;
We dig de row dem eben in a line,
An' keep it clean—den so it *mus'* look fine.

You tas'e petater an' you say it sweet,
But you no know how hard we wuk fe it;
Yet still de hardship always melt away
Wheneber it come roun' to reapin' day.

---

17. A piece of humourous exaggeration: "When you see the potatoes tearing up the
ground in their rapid growth you will run to save yourself from being caught and entangled
in the vines."
18. You are laughing, sir—perhaps you think I am exaggerating.
19. Less than that = be otherwise.
20. We work as well as we possibly can.

Me Bannabees[1]

Run ober mango trees,
    'Pread chock[2] to kitchen doo',
Watch de blue bannabees,
    Look how it ben' down low!

De blossom draw de bees
    Same how de soup draw man;[3]
Some call it "broke-pot" peas,
    It caan' bruk we bu'n-pan.[4]

Wha' sweet so when it t'ick?[5]
    Though some call it goat-tud,[6]
Me all me finger lick,
    An' yet no chew me cud.[7]

A mumma plant[8] de root
    One day jes' out o' fun;[9]
But now look 'pon de fruit,
    See wha' de "mek fun"[10] done.

I jam de 'tick dem 'traight
    Soon as it 'tart fe 'pread,[11]
An begin count de date
    Fe when de pod fe shed.[12]

---

1. A corruption of Bonavist, a climbing bean or pea.
2. Right up.
3. The blossom attracts bees, just as the soup made from the peas attracts man.
4. It can't break our burn-pain—a tall saucepan.
5. What is so good as this soup, when it is thick?
6. Goat droppings—the name of a poisonous plant, somewhat resembling bannabees.
7. Because I haven't yet got my belly full: see below.
8. It was mamma who planted.
9. With no serious purpose.
10. To make fun = to trifle.
11. As soon as it began to spread.
12. When the pod will be formed.

CLAUDE MCKAY

Me watch de vine dem grow,
    S'er[13] t'row dung a de root:
Crop time look fe me slow,
    De bud tek long fe shoot.

But so de day did come,
    I 'crub de bu'n-pan bright,
An' tu'n down 'pon it[14] from
    De marnin' till de night.

An' Lard I me belly swell,
    No 'cause de peas no good,
But me be'n tek[15] a 'pell
    Mo' dan a giant would.

Yet eben after dat
    Me nyam[16] it wid a will,
'Causen it mek me fat;
    So I wi' lub it still.

Caan' talk about gungu,
    Fe me it is no peas
Cockstone might do fe you,
    Me want me bannabees.

---

13. Sister.
14. The soup.
15. Did take.
16. I ate.

Lub O' Mine

Darlin', though you lub me still,
    I feel it so,
To t'ink dat we neber will
    Meet soon, you know;

Eben when you tell me say[1]
    Dat your dear heart[2]
Did grow 'tronger ebery day
    An' hate fe part.

Feelin' all you' lub for me,
    I t'ink[3] you press
Your heart, as it use' to be,[4]
    Upon me breas'.

Lubin' you wid all me soul,
    De lub is such
Dat it beat out blood,[5]—de whole,[6]
    An' dat is much.

Lubin' you as you go 'long
    In a you walk;[7]
Also when you chune[8] a song,
    An' as you talk.

---

1. Although you do tell me. The word 'say' is redundant.
2. Love.
3. Imagine.
4. As formerly.
5. Beats out relations—*i.e.*, makes relations nothing.
6. Father and mother and all.
7. In your walk.
8. Tune = sung.

CLAUDE MCKAY

An' a so I hate fe see[9]
    You go astray
In those t'ings dat you and me
    Can cast away.[10]

Lub, I dyin'[11] fe you' smile,
    An' some sweet news
Dat can cheer me heart awhile
    Fe wha' it lose.

Lub me, darlin'—lub, aldough
    You are now gone:
You can never leave me so—
    Friendless-alone.

---

9. And I so hate to see.
10. Need not do.
11. I am dying.

Taken Aback

Let me go, Joe, for I want go[1] home:
    Can't stan' wid you,[2]
    For pa might go[3] come;
An' if him only hab him rum,
I don't know whatever I'll do.[4]

I must go now, for it's gettin' night
    I am afraid,
    An' tis not moonlight:
Give me de last hug, an' do it tight;
Me pa gwin' go knock off me head.[5]

No, Joe, don't come!—you will keep me late,
    An' pa might be
    In him[6] sober state;
Him might get vex'[7] an' lock up de gate,
Den what will becomin' of me?

Go wid *you*, Joe?—you don't lub me den!
    I shame'[8] o' you—
    Gals caan'[9] trust you men!
An' I b'en tekin' you fe me frien';[10]
Good-night, Joe, you've proven untrue.

---

1. To go.
2. I can't stay with you.
3. A redundant word, unaccented.
4. If he chances to be in liquor.
5. My paper is going to go (and) knock off my head. The *o* in "going" is pronounced very short, making it sound like a *w*.
6. His.
7. Vexed.
8. Am ashamed.
9. Can't.
10. And I've been taking you for my friend.

CLAUDE MCKAY

JIM AT SIXTEEN

Corpy,[1] it pinch me so,
    De bloomin' ole handcuff;
A dun no warra mek[2]
    You put it on so rough.

Many a póliceman
    Hab come to dis before;
Dem slip same like a[3] me,
    An' pass t'rough lock-up door.[4]

Mumma, no bodder[5] cry,
    It should an[6] hotter be;
I wouldn' heed you when
    You use'[7] fe talk to me.

I run[8] away from you
    Same as I tu'n out school,[9]
'Caus'n a didn' want
    To stan' under no rule.[10]

An' though you send[11] fe me,
    A wouldn' face de home;
Yet still dem[12] find you quick
    Same as de trouble come.[13]

---

1. Corporal.
2. I don't know what made.
3. This intrusive "a" is common. "Like" has the pronunciation of French *lac*.
4. The door of the lock-up.
5. Do not bother (trouble) to cry—*i.e.*, do not cry.
6. Intrusive again.
7. Used.
8. Ran.
9. As soon as I left school.
10. To be under discipline.
11. Sent.
12. The police.
13. When the trouble came.

Mumma, I know quite well
    You' lub fe me is 'trong;
Yet still you don't a go
    Join wid me in a wrong.[14]

An' so I won't beg you
    To pay[15] fe me today;
I'll bear me punishment,[16]
    'Twill teach me to obey

          * * * * * * * * * *

Mumma, you' Jim get 'way
    An' come back home[17] to you,
An' ask[18] you to forgive
    Him all o' whe' him do.[19]

I want you to feget
    Dat I disgrace de name,
An' cause de ole fam'ly[20]
    To look 'pon me wid shame.

You come an' beg de judge
    Before dem call fe me,[21]
An' walk by de back gate,
    T'inkin' I wouldn' see.

But 'fore him let me go,
    Him lectur' me, mumma,
Tellin' me how I mus'
    Try no fe bruk de law.[22]

---

14. You are not going to back me up in wrongdoing.
15. The fine.
16. And go to prison.
17. Has got off an comes home.
18. Asks.
19. All he has done.
20. Pronounce *fahmly*.
21. You came and begged the magistrate before my case was brought on.
22. Telling me I must take care not to break the law. Pronounce *lah*.

         CLAUDE MCKAY

Mumma, I feel it, but
    No eye-water caan' drop:
Yet I wish dat it could,
    For me breat' partly 'top.[23]

So, mumma, I come back
    Again to be your boy,
An' ever as before
    To fill you' heart wid joy.

NOTE BY THE AUTHOR: On Friday I went to Court on duty for the third time since my enlistment. I happened to escort a prisoner, a stalwart young fellow, and as I was putting on the handcuff, which was rather small, it pinched him badly, making a raw wound. And yet he was so patient, saying he knew that I could not help it. Although it was accidentally done, I felt so sad and ashamed. The above poem grew out of this incident.

23. He means, that the lamp in his throat is more painful than tears.

WHE' FE DO?[1]

Life will continue so for aye,
Some people sad, some people gay,
Some mockin'[2] life while udders pray;
But we mus' fashion-out we way
An' sabe a mite fe rainy day—
    All we can do.

We needn' fold we han' an' cry,
Nor vex we heart wid groan and sigh;
De best we can do is fe try
To fight de despair drawin' nigh:
Den we might conquer by an' by—
    Dat we might do.

We hab to batter[3] in de sun,
An' dat isn't a little fun,
For Lard! 'tis hellish how it bu'n:
Still dere's de big wul' to live do'n—
    So whe' fe do?

We nigger hab a tas'[4] fe do,
To conquer prejudice dat[5] due
To obeah,[6] an' t'ings not a few
Dat keep we progress back fe true,[7]—
    But whe' fe do?

---

1. What to do?—equivalent to "What can't be cured, must be endured." The *e* whe' is the French é.
2. Making mock at.
3. Labour and sweat; swink.
4. Task.
5. That's.
6. Sorcery and magic.
7. Very much.

CLAUDE MCKAY

We've got to wuk wid might an' main,
To use we han' an' use we brain,
To toil an' worry, 'cheme an' 'train[8]
Fe t'ings that bring more loss dan gain;
To stan' de sun an bear de rain,
An' suck we bellyful o' pain
Widouten cry[9] nor yet complain—
    For dat caan'[10] do.

And though de wul' is full o' wrong,
Dat caan' prevent we sing we song
All de day as we wuk along—
    Whe' else fe do?

We happy in de hospital;[11]
We happy when de rain deh fall;[12]
We happy though de baby bawl
Fe food dat we no hab at all;[13]
We happy when Deat' angel call[14]
Fe full[15] we cup of joy wid gall:
Our fait' in this life is not small—
    De best to do.

An' da's[16] de way we ought to live,
For pain an' such[17] we shouldn' grieve,
But tek de best dat Nature give—
    Da's whe' fe do.

---

8. Scheme and strain.
9. Without crying.
10. Can't = won't.
11. All the lines of this stanza end with the sound *ahl*.
12. Is falling.
13. Don't have at all = haven't got.
14. Death's angel calls.
15. Fill.
16. That's.
17. The like.

God mek de wul' fe black an' white;
We'll wuk on in de glad sunlight,
Keep toilin' on wid all our might,
An' sleep in peace when it is night:
We must strive on to gain de height,
Aldough it may not be in sight;
An' yet perhaps de blessed right
Will never conquer in de fight—
    Still, whe' fe do?

We'll try an' live as any man,[18]
An' fight de wul' de best we can,
E'en though it hard fe understan'—
    Whe' we mus' do.

For da's de way o' dis ya wul';[19]
It's snap an' bite, an' haul an' pull,
An' we all get we bellyful—
    But whe' fe do?

---

18. As others do, who make a good fight.
19. Of this (here) world.

           CLAUDE MCKAY

King Banana

Green mancha[1] mek[2] fe naygur man;
    Wha' sweet so when it roas'?
Some boil it in a big black pan,
    It sweeter in a toas'.[3]

A buccra fancy[4] when it ripe,
    Dem use it ebery day;
It scarcely give dem belly-gripe,
    Dem eat it diffran' way.[5]

Out yonder see somoke[6] a rise,
    An' see de fire wicket;[7]
Deh go'p to heaben wid de nize[8]
    Of hundred t'ousan' cricket.

De black moul' lie do'n quite prepare'
    Fe feel de hoe an' rake;
De fire bu'n, and it tek care
    Fe mek de wo'm[9] dem wake.

Wha' lef fe buccra teach again
    Dis time about plantation?
Dere's not'in' dat can beat de plain
    Good ole-time cultibation.

---

1. Corruption of "Martinique," the best variety of banana in Jamaica.
2. Is (or was) made.
3. In a toast = toasted.
4. It is buccra's fancy, *i.e.*, the white man likes it.
5. In a different way : not so much at a time as we eat.
6. This lengthening of a monosyllable into a dissyllable is common.
7. Wicked.
8. It goes up to heaven with the noise, etc. This is an excellent simile, as those acquainted with tropical crickets will know.
9. Worms, *i.e.*, grubs.

Banana dem fat all de same[10]
    From bunches big an' 'trong;
Pure nine-han' bunch a car' de fame,[11]—
    Ole met'od all along.

De cuttin' done same ole-time way,
    We wrap dem in a trash,
An' pack dem neatly in a dray
    So tight dat dem can't mash.

We re'ch:[12] banana finish sell;[13]
    Den we 'tart back fe home:
Some hab money in t'read-bag[14] well,
    Some spen' all in a rum.

Green mancha mek fe naygur man,
    It mek fe him all way;[15]
Our islan' is banana lan',
    Banana car' de sway.[16]

---

10. In spite of primitive methods of cultivation the bananas are just as plump.
11. The nine-hand and only (*pure*) nine-hand bunches—none smaller, that is—grown by this old method have a fine reputation.
12. Reach our journey's end.
13. The selling of bananas is over.
14. Bag secured by a thread (string) round the mouth.
15. In every way. He can eat it or sell it.
16. Carries the sway, *i.e.*, is Jamaica's mainstay.

PLEADING

...nie, only tell me, dear,

...old

When my lub is bold;

Do not mek dis burning heart o' mine get drear,
    Tek it for your own,
    For 'tis yours alone.

I hab ever lub'd you from I saw[1] your face
    On dat Monday morn
    'Mongst de peas an' corn:
Lightly did you trip along wid yout'ful grace,
    Wid de kerchief red
    Wound about your head.

Durin' de revival[2] we b'en use' fe pray,
    Spirit we b'en hab,
    How we use' fe sob!
Yet how soon did all of it from we get 'way![3]
    Lub kiver de whole,
    We feget we "soul."

Though I could'n' see you when you younger b'en,
    It was better so,
    For we older grow,
An' I can protect you now from udder men,
    If you'll only be
    Fe me one,[4] Joanie.

How I saw you proudly draw up to your height—
    As we strolled along
    Gay in laugh an' song,

---

1. From the moment that I saw.
2. At the revival meetings those who "have the Spirit" give grunting sobs.
3. Go away, pass away.
4. Mine alone.

by de peenies[5] sheddin' greenish light'—
Cos my lips did miss,[6]
Stealin' one lee[7] kiss!

'Member you de days down by de river-side,
    I prevented you
    Your washin' to do,
Teasin' you at times till you got vex' an' cried,
    An' I try de while
    To coax you fe smile?

Joanie, when you were me own a[8] true sweetheart,
    I lived in de air
    'Douten[9] t'ought of care,
Thinkin', o me Joan, dat' nuttin' could we[10] part,
    Naught to mek me fear
    Fe me own a dear.

When in church on Sunday days we use' fe sit,
    You dressed in light pink,
    How we used fe wink!
Wha' de parson say we cared for not a bit,
    Nuttin' could remove
    Our sweet t'oughts from love.

I am thinkin', Joanie, when de nights were lone,
    An' you were afraid
    Of each darkened shade,
An' I use' fe guide you over river-stone,[11]
    How you trusted me
    Fe care[12] you, Joanie.

---

5. Fire-flies.
6. Make a mistake.
7. Little.
8. There is a delicious caressing sound about this intrusive "a."
9. Withouten, without.
10. Us.
11. The stepping stones in the river.
12. Look after.

CLAUDE MCKAY

'Member you de time when many days passed by,
    An' I didn' come
    To your hill-side home,
How you wrote those sad, sad letters to know why,
    Till I comfort gave
    To my Joanie brave?

In those happy days, me Joan, you loved me then,
    An' I t'ought dat you
    Would be ever true;
Never dreamed you would forsake me for strange men,
    Who caan' lub you so
    Much as thrown-up Joe.

Joanie, fickle Joanie, give up Squire's son;
    You wi' soon hate him
    An' his silly whim,
An' your heart wi' yearn fe me when I am gone;
    So, 'fo' 'tis too late,
    Come back to your mate.

Joanie, when you're tired of dat worthless man,
    You can come back still
    Of your own free will:
Nummo[13] girl dis true, true heart will understan';
    I wi' live so-so,[14]
    Broken-hearted Joe.

An', Joan, in de days fe come I know you'll grieve
    For de foolishniss
    Dat you now call bliss:
Dere's no wrong you done me I would not forgive;
    But you choice[15] your way,
    So, me Joan, good-day!

13. No other girl can understand.
14. Alone.
15. Choose, have chosen.

The Biter Bit

"Ole woman a swea' fe eat calalu:[1] *calalu a swea' fe wuk him*[2] *gut."*

—Jamaica Proverb

Corn an' peas growin' t'ick an' fas'
Wid nice blade peepin' t'rough de grass;
An' ratta[3] a from dem hole a peep,
T'ink all de corn *dem* gwin' go reap.

Ole woman sit by kitchen doo'
Is watchin' calalu a grow,
An' all de time a t'inking dat
She gwin' go nyam dem when dem fat.[4]

But calalu, grow'n' by de hut,
Is swearin' too fe wuk him gut;
While she, like some, t'ink[5] all is right
When dey are in some corner tight.

Peas time come roun'[6] —de corn is lef;
An' ratta now deh train himse'f
Upon de cornstalk dem a' night
Fe when it fit to get him bite.[7]

De corn-piece lie do'n all in blue,[8]
An' all de beard dem floatin' too
Amongst de yellow grain so gay,[9]
Dat you would watch dem a whole day.

---

1. Spinach.
2. His = her.
3. The rats.
4. Juicy.
5. Thinks; but it also means "think," and so equally applies to the plural subject.
6. The time for harvesting the peas arrives.
7. And (every) rat now practises climbing the cornstalks at night, so that he may get his bite when the corn is ripe.
8. This refers to the bluish leaf of the maize.
9. Supply "all this makes so pretty a picture."

CLAUDE MCKAY

An' ratta look at ebery one,
Swea'in' dat dem not gwin' lef none;[10]
But Quaco know a t'ing or two,
An' swear say[11] dat dem won't go so.

So him go get a little meal
An' somet'ing good fe those dat steal,
An' mix dem up an' 'pread dem out
For people possess fas' fas' mout'.[12]

Now ratta, comin' from dem nes',
See it an' say "Dis food is bes';"
Dem nyam an' stop, an' nyam again,
An' soon lie do'n, rollin' in pain.

---

10. They are not going to leave any.
11. "Say" is redundant : it is tacked closely to "swear."
12. For those who are too quick with their mouths.

Out of Debt

De Christmas is finish';
It was rather skinnish,[1]
Yet still we are happy, an' so needn' fret,
For dinner is cookin',
An' baby is lookin'
An' laughin'; she knows dat her pa owe no debt.

De pas' hab de debtor,[2]
 An' we cannot get her[3]
To come back an' grin at us as in time gone:
Dere's no wine fe breakfas',[4]
An' no one fe mek fuss,
We all is contented fe suck one dry bone.

No two bit o' brater[5]
Wid shopkeeper Marter,
I feel me head light sittin' down by me wife;
No weight lef behin' me
No gungu[6] a line fe
De man who was usual[7] to worry me life.

We're now out o' season,[8]
But dat is no reason
Why we shan't be happy wid heart free and light:
We feel we are better
Dan many dat fetter
Wid burden dey shoulder to mek Christmas bright.

---

1. The fare was rather meagre.
2. We were in debt last Christmas, but now are free.
3. The past.
4. The midday meal.
5. Shopkeeper Marter and I are no longer two brothers : meaning, I am not always going into his shop, and so keeping in debt. Pronounce *brather*.
6. Friends plant their gungu (Congo peas) together, and, in picking the crop, are not particular about the line between their properties. When they cease to be friends, they have *no gungo a line*. The phrase is equivalent to "to have no truck with."
7. Pronounce without sounding the second *u*. Was usual = used.
8. Past Christmas.

Some 'crape out de cupboard,
Not 'memberin' no wud[9]
Dat say about fegettin' when rainy day:
  It comes widout warning
  'Fo' daylight a[10] marnin',
An', wakin', de blue cloud ta'n black dat was gay.

  De days dat gwin' follow
  No more will be hollow,
Like some dat come after de Christmas before:
  We'll lay by some money
  An' lick at de honey,[11]
An' neber will need to lock up our front door.[12]

  Jes'[13] look at de brightness
  Of dat poor an' sightless
Old man on de barrel a playin' de flute:
  Wha' mek him so joyful?
  His lap is of toy full,
A pick'ninny play wid de patch on his suit.

  Ours too de same blessin',
  An' we've learn' a lesson
We should have been learnin' from years long ago:
  A Christmas 'dout pleasure[14]
  Gave dat darlin' treasure,[15]
An' duty to Milly is all dat we owe.

---

9. Entirely oblivious of the proverb (word) which tells us not to forget to make provision for the rainy day.
10. In the.
11. Enjoy the pleasure it brings.
12. Against the bailiff.
13. Just.
14. Without pleasure, *i.e.*, a sober and quiet Christmas.
15. Our little pickny.

THE HERMIT

Far in de country let me hide myself
From life's sad pleasures an' de greed of pelf,
Dwellin' wid Nature primitive an' rude,
Livin' a peaceful life of solitude.

Dere by de woodland let me build my home
Where tropic roses[1] ever are in bloom,
An' t'rough de wild cane[2] growin' thick and tall
Rushes in gleeful mood de waterfall.

Roof strong enough to keep out season rain,[3]
Under whose eaves loved swallows will be fain
To build deir nests, an' deir young birdlings rear
Widouten have de least lee t'ought of fear.[4]

An' in my study I shall view de wul',
An' learn of all its doin's to de full;
List to de woodland creatures' music sweet—
Sad, yet contented in my lone retreat.

---

1. In Jamaica any showy or sweet flower is called a rose.
2. *Arundo Donax.*
3. The heavy rains of May and October were called "season rains."
4. Without having the smallest (least little) thought of fear.

Fetchin' Water

Watch how dem touris' like fe look
　　Out 'pon me little daughter,
Whenever fe her tu'n[1] to cook
　　Or fetch a pan of water:
　　　　De sight look gay;
　　　　Dat is one way,
　　　　But I can tell you say,[2]
'Nuff rock'tone in de sea, yet none
But those 'pon lan' know 'bouten sun.[3]

De pickny comin' up de hill,
　　Fightin' wid heavy gou'd,[4]
Won't say it sweet[5] him, but he will
　　Complain about de load:
　　　　Him feel de weight,
　　　　Dem[6] watch him gait;
　　　　It's so some of de great
High people fabour t'ink[7] it sweet
Fe batter[8] in de boilin' heat.

Dat boy wid de karásene[9] pan,
　　Sulky down to him toe,
His back was rollin' in a san',[10]
　　For him pa mek him crow:[11]
　　　　Him feel it bad,
　　　　Near mek him mad,

---

1. It is her turn.
2. The "say" is redundant.
3. In allusion to the Jamaica proverb, "Rock'tone (stone) a river bottom no feel sun hot."
4. Struggling under his head-load—a gourd (calabash) filled with water.
5. Is agreeable to.
6. The tourists watch his upright carriage.
7. Favour think = seem to think.
8. Labour and sweat; toil and moil.
9. The favourite receptacle for water is a four-gallon kerosene tin (pan.)
10. In the sand.
11. Cry out.

But teach him[12] he's a lad;
Go disobey him fader wud,[13]
When he knows dat his back would sud![14]

But Sarah Jane she wus 'an all,
    For she t'row 'way[15] de pan,
An' jam her back agains' de wall
    Fe fight her mumma Fan:
       Feelin' de pinch,
       She mek a wrinch
       An' get 'way; but de wench
Try fe put shame upon her ma,
Say dat she cook de bittle raw.[16]

Dis water-fetchin' sweet dem though
    When day mek up dem min',
An' 'nuff o' dem 'tart out fe go,
    An' de weader is fine:
       De pan might leak,
       Dem don't a 'peak,
       Nor eben try fe seek
Some clay or so[17] to mek it soun';
Dem don't care ef dem wet all roun'.

Dén all 'bout de road dem 'catter
    Marchin' álong quite at ease;
Dat time listen to deir chatter,
    Talkin' anyt'ing dem please:
       Dem don't a fear,

---

12. But it will teach him.
13. What?—disobey his father's orders?
14. Get a lathering.
15. Threw down.
16. Said that she cooked the victual raw, *i.e.*, only half cooked it.
17. Or something.

Neider a care,
For who can interfere?
T'ree mile—five, six tu'n,[18]—an' neber[19]
W'ary, but could do it[20] for eber.

---

18. Turns, *i.e.*, journeys to the spring and back.
19. For rhythm, read thus : T'ree mile—five, six—tu'n, an'—neber.
20. Pronounce *dweet*.

School-Teacher Nell's Lub-Letter

If you promise to lub me alway,
    I will foreber be true,
An' you don't mek me sorry[1] I de day
    Dat I give myself to you.

How I 'member de night when we meet,[2]
    An' chat fe de first time of lub!
I go home, an' den neber could eat
    None o' de plateful o' grub.

An' de day it was empty to me,
    Wakin', but dreamin' of you,
While de school it was dull as could be,
    An' me hate me wuk fe do.[3]

Oh, I knew of your lub long before
    My school friends tell[4] me of it,
And I watch at you from de school door,
    When you pass to de cockpit.[5]

Den I hear too dat you use' fe talk,
Say,[6] if you caan' ketch me dark night,
You would sure ketch me as me deh walk[7]
In a de[8] open moonlight.

An' you' wud come to pass[9] very soon,
    For scarcely a mont' did gone

---

1. Make me regret.
2. How well I remember the night we met.
3. I hated the doing of my work.
4. Told.
5. A natural depression in the ground, in the vicinity of the author's home, bears this name.
6. Used to (talk and) say.
7. You would be sure to catch me as I walked.
8. In the.
9. And your word came to pass.

When de light of de star an' de moon
    Shine[10] bright as we kiss all alone.

I can neber remember de times
    Ma scolded her little Nell;[11]
All day her tongue wuks like de chimes
    Dat come from de old school-bell.

I have given up school-life fe you:
    Sweetheart, my all[12] is your own;
Den say you will ever be true,
    An' live fe you' Nellie alone.

---

10. Shone.
11. I cannot count the number of scoldings I have had from mamma.
12. Whole self.

NELLIE WHITE

(An Answer To The Foregoing)

Sweetheart, I have loved you well,
More than dis lee tongue can tell,
An' you need not hab no fear,
For I'll marry you, my dear.

What are you talkin' about?
Don't say that I'll play you out;[1]
Swif' ole Time, me Nell, will prove
Dat 'tis you alone I love.

Cry not, except 'tis for joy;
Can't you trus' dis big-heart boy?
Nell, I hate fe see you weep;
Tek my heart, an' go to sleep.

How could I deceive you, Nell?
Don't I love you much too well?
Could I fool dat plump black cheek?
Don't cry, darlin'—look up—speak I

Nellie of the pretty feet
An' the palm-like shape so neat,
I have eyes to see but you;
Darling, trust me to be true!

Nell, me dear, you need not fret,
For you are my food, my breat';
Trust me, trust me, Nellie White,
Kiss me, lee sweetheart—good-night!

---

1. False.

Retribution

De mule dem in de pasture an' de donkey 'pon red
    ground',[1]
An' we boys mus' ketch dem all befo' de evenin'
    sun go do'n;
De tas'[2] it isn't easy for de whole o' dem can run,
        An' grass-lice[3] lie do'n set.[4]

Grass-lice dat mek you trimble long time[5] more
    dan when you meet
A man dat mean to fight you who you know you
    cannot beat;
Dem mek you feel you' blood crawl from you' head
    do'n to you' feet,
        An' wish dat you b'en[6] wet.

An', like a 'pite,[7] see all de mule a 'ketter t'rough de
    grass,
So chupidly a-followin' de foolish ole jackass;
But when you hea' we ketch dem, we wi' serve dem
    such a sauce
        By ridin' dem to deat'!

We breat' is partly givin' out[8] as up de hill we go
    up;
De beast dem seem to understan' say "Day longer
    'an rope,"[9]

---

1. Poor patchy land with open spaces of red earth.
2. Task.
3. Small ticks.
4. Waiting for us.
5. Long time = much.
6. Had been, were.
7. As though to spite us.
8. Three parts gone.
9. Ro-op, in two syllables. The proverb means, "I'll be even with you."

An' dat de night wi' come befo' we ketch dem is
    deir hope;
        But we shall conquer yet.

For though dem t'ink dem hab some sense, dem
    all run right between
De rocky road above de swamp, where it hab eber
    been
Our luck to nab dem in de trap dat neber can be
    seen
        By dem—Dey're in de net!

We hab dem pullin' on de bit as we race mile 'pon
    mile,
An' grass-lice in we back a crawl an' 'ting us all de
    while;
But blood is drippin' from dem mout', twill teach
    dem not fe[10] vile,
        We'll race dem out o' breat'.

---

10. To be.

To E.M.E.

You see[1] me smile: but what is it?
A sweetened pain—a laughing fit—
    A little honeyed dart,
    That, passing, stabs my heart,
Yet mek me glad a bit.

You see me dance: 'twas but my feet,
You should have heard my heart a beat!
    For non o' it was real:
    It be'n a priceless[2] sale
Of bitter for a sweet.

Dis laughin' face!—'tis full o' joy
Because it is a baby's toy;[3]
    But when de child is gone
    An' the darkness comes on,
'Twill be anudder boy.[4]

You hear me sing: what is de tune?
De song of one that's dyin' soon,
    A whirlin', tossin' life
    Flung on de wul' of strife;
I call it 'debil's boon.'

De many pleasures? Wha's de gain?
I'll tell you of a grindin' pain
    Dat companies de birt',
    An' runs[5] wid vengeance[6] mirt'
De life, till it is slain.

---

1. Saw.
2. Profitless.
3. The speaker has a baby on his knee.
4. I shall look very different.
5. Chase, hunts.
6. Vengeful.

Why do I sleep? My eyes know why,
Same how a life knows why it die:[7]
    Dey sleep on in distress,
    Knowin' not why dey res',
But feelin' why dey cry.

I'm hungry now, so eat once mo',
E'en though I'll soon be like befo';
    For, as in udder t'ings,
    De seemin' pleasure clings,
De cravin' has no cure.

It always seem so strange to me,
Dat *you* can satisfy[8] to be
    A life whose daily food
    Is pain: de only good,
Deat' dat will set it free.

7. My eyes no more know why, than a life knows why it dies.
8. Be content.

Hard Times

De mo' me wuk, de mo' time hard,
   I don't know what fe do;
I ben' me knee an' pray to Gahd,
   Yet t'ings same as befo'.

De taxes knockin' at me door,
   I hear de bailiff's v'ice;
Me wife is sick, can't get no cure,
   But gnawin' me like mice.[1]

De picknies hab to go to school
   Widout a bite fe taste;
And I am working like a mule,
While buccra, sittin' in de cool,
   Hab 'nuff nenyam fe waste.[2]

De clodes is' tearin' off dem back
   When money seems noa mek;
A man can't eben ketch a mac,[3]
   Care how him 'train him neck.[4]

De peas won't pop,[5] de corn can't grow,
   Poor people face[6] look sad;
Dat Gahd would cuss de lan' I'd know,
   For black naygur too bad.

---

1. Trying to get money from me.
2. Food and to spare.
3. Shilling : short for macaroni.
4. However hard he may strain his neck. "Care how"—I don't care how,—no matter how.
5. Spring.
6. People's faces.

I won't gib up, I won't say die,
    For all[7] de time is hard;
Aldough de wul' soon en', I'll try
My wutless[8] best as time goes by,
    An' trust on in me Gahd.

---

7. Although.
8. Worthless : meaning, "I'll try my very best, poor as that may be."

CLAUDE MCKAY

CUDJOE FRESH FROM DE LECTURE

'Top *one* minute, Cous' Jarge, an' sit do'n 'pon de
    grass,
An' mek a[1] tell you 'bout de news I hear at las',
How de buccra te-day tek time an' begin teach
All of us dat was deh[2] in a clear open speech.

You miss somet'ing fe true, but a wi' mek you
    know,
As much as how a can, how de business a go:
Him tell us 'bout we self, an' mek we fresh[3] again,
An' talk about de wul' from commencement to en'.

Me look 'pon me black 'kin, an' so me head grow
    big,
Aldough me heaby han' dem hab fe plug[4] an' dig;
For ebery single man, no car'[5] about dem rank,
Him bring us ebery one an' put 'pon de same plank.

Say, parson do de same?[6] Yes, in a 'dift'ren' way,
For parson tell us how de whole o' we are clay;
An' lookin' close at t'ings, we hab to pray quite
    hard
Fe swaller wha' him say an' don't t'ink bad o'
    Gahd.

But dis man tell us 'traight 'bout how de whole
    t'ing came,
An' show us widout doubt how Gahd was not fe
    blame;

---

1. Make I = let me.
2. There.
3. Over: meaning, "He gave us a new view of our origin, and explained that we did not come from Adam and Eve, but by evolution."
4. Plough, *i.e.*, pick up the ground with a pickaxe.
5. Care: no matter what their rank.
6. Do you say that parson does the same?

How change cause eberyt'ing fe mix up 'pon de eart',
An' dat most hardship come t'rough accident o'
    birt'.

Him show us all a sort[7] o' funny 'keleton,
Wid names I won't remember under dis ya sun;
Animals queer to deat'[8], dem bone, teet', an'
    head-skull,
All dem so dat did live in a de ole-time wul'.

No 'cos say we get cuss mek fe we 'kin come so,
But fe all t'ings come 'quare, same so it was to go:[9]
Seems our lan'[10] must ha' been a bery low-do'n
    place,
Mek it tek such long time in tu'ning out a race.

Yes, from monkey we spring: I believe ebery
    wud;
It long time better dan f'go say we come from
    mud:
No need me keep back part, me hab not'in' fe
    gain;
It's ebery man dat born—de buccra mek it
    plain.

It really strange how some o' de lan' dem advance;
Man power in some ways is nummo soso chance;[11]
But suppose eberyt'ing could tu'n right upside
    down,
Den p'raps we'd be on top an' givin' some one
    houn'.[12]

---

7. All sorts.
8. The queerest animals.
9. It is not because we are cursed (Gen. ix. 25) that our skin is dark; but so that things might come square, there had to be black and white.
10. Africa.
11. No more than pure chance.
12. Hound: equivalent to the English slang phrase, "giving some one beans."

Yes, Cous' Jarge, slabery hot fe dem dat gone
    befo':
We gettin' better times, for those days we no
    know;[13]
But I t'ink it do good, tek we from Africa
An' lan' us in a blessed place as dis a ya.[14]

Talk 'bouten Africa, we would be deh till now,
Maybe same half-naked—all day dribe buccra cow,
An' tearin' t'rough de bush wid all de monkey dem,
Wile an' uncibilise',[15] an' neber comin' tame.

l Ief' quite 'way from wha' we be'n deh talk about,[16]
Yet still a couldn' help—de wuds come to me
    mout';
Just like how yeas' get strong an' something fly de
    cark,[17]
Same way me feelings grow, so I was boun' fe talk.

Yet both horse partly[18] runnin' in de selfsame
    gallop,
For it is nearly so de way de buccra pull up:
Him say, how de wul' stan', dat right will neber be,
But wrong will eber gwon[19] till dis wul' en' fe we.

---

13. Do not know: have no experience of.
14. This here.
15. Wild and uncivilised.
16. I have run right away from what we were talking about.
17. Makes the cork fly.
18. Almost.
19. Go on.

DE DAYS DAT ARE GONE

I T'ink of childhood days again,
    An' wish dat I was free
To res' me baby head once more
    Upon me mudder's knee:
If we had power to change dis life
    An' live it back again,
We would be children all de time
    Nor fret at childhood's pain.

I look on my school life of old,
    Dem sweet days dat are pas',
An' wonder how I'd wish[1] to see
    Those dear times en' at las':
It was because I was a boy,
    An' knew not what b'en good;
All time I tas'e de supple-jack,[2]
    Bein' I was so rude.

An' o' de marnings when I woke,
    'Fo' you can see you' han',
I mek me way on to de spring
    Fe full[3] me bucket-pan:
I t'ought ofttimes dat it was hard
    For me to wake so soon;
Dere was no star fe light de way,
    Much more[4] de white roun' moon.

Still, childhood pain could neber las',
    An' I remember yet
De many sorrows 'cross me pat'[5]
    Dat neber mek me fret:

---

1. I could wish.
2. A cane.
3. Fill.
4. Less.
5. Across the path.

CLAUDE MCKAY

But now me joys are only few,
    I live because I'm boun',
An' try fe mek my life of use
    Though pain lie all aroun'.

Reveille Soun'in'

Reveille! de reveille soun',
    Depôt p'liceman mus' wake up;[1]
Some mus' dress fe go to town,
    Some to Parade fe shake-up.[2]

You lazy ones can lay down still,
    We have no time fe dat;
De wake-up[3] comin' roun', an' you'll
    Jump as you feel de cat.

For soon de half pas' dress[4] will blow
    Fe we to go a-drillin';
De time is bery short, an' so
    We mus' be quick an' willin'.

A marnin' bade is sweet fe true,[5]
    But we mus' quick fe done;
It col' dough,[6] so it's only few
    Can stan' it how it bu'n.[7]

'Tis quarter warnin'[8] soun'in' now,
    Our arms mus' clean an' soun';
We will ketch 'port[9] ef we allow
    A speck fe lodge aroun'.

---

1. Read thus: De—pôt p'lice—man mus'—wake up.
2. Drill.
3. The sergeant with his cane.
4. The 5.30 bugle.
5. A morning bathe is very, very delicious.
6. It's cold enough.
7. Can stand the burning *i.e.*, the chill.
8. The 5.45 bugle.
9. Get reported.

CLAUDE MCKAY

Tip[10] blow yet? good Lard! hear "fall in,"
   Must double 'pon de grass;
I didn' know de las' call be'n
   Deh blow on us so fas'.

---

10. A short sharp bugle-call, to summon the men before the "fall in."

OLD ENGLAND

I've a longin' in me dept's of heart dat I can
    conquer not,
'Tis a wish dat I've been havin' from since I could
    form a t'o't,[1]
'Tis to sail athwart the ocean an' to hear de billows
    roar,
When dem ride aroun' de steamer, when dem beat
    on England's shore.

Just to view de homeland England, in de streets
    of London walk,
An' to see de famous sights dem 'bouten which
    dere's so much talk,
An' to watch de fact'ry chimneys pourin' smoke up
    to de sky,
An' to see de matches-children, dat I hear 'bout,
    passin' by.

I would see Saint Paul's Cathedral, an' would hear
    some of de great
Learnin' comin' from de bishops, preachin' relics
    of old fait';
I would ope me mout' wid wonder at de massive
    organ soun',
An' would 'train me eyes to see de beauty Iyin'
    all aroun'.

I'd go to de City Temple, where de 'old fait' is
    a wreck,
An' de parson is a-preachin' views dat most folks
    will not tek;
I'd go where de men of science meet togeder in
    deir hall,
To give light unto de real truths, to obey king
    Reason's call.

---

1. Thought.

I would view Westminster Abbey, where de great
    of England sleep,
An' de solemn marble statues o'er deir ashes vigil
    keep;
I would see immortal Milton an' de wul'-famous
    Shakespeare,
Past'ral Wordswort', gentle Gray, an' all de great
    souls buried dere.

I would see de ancient chair where England's
    kings deir crowns put on,
Soon to lay dem by again when all de vanity is
    done;
An' I'd go to view de lone spot where in peaceful
    solitude
Rests de body of our Missis Queen[2], Victoria de
    Good.
An' dese places dat I sing of now shall afterwards
    impart
All deir solemn sacred beauty to a weary searchin'
    heart;
So I'll rest glad an' contented in me min'[3] for
    evermore,
When I sail across de ocean back to my own
    native shore.

---

2. Always called so in Jamaica.
3. Mind.

DAT DIRTY RUM

If you *must* drink it, do not come
An' chat up in my face;
I hate to see de dirty rum,
Much more to know de tas'e.

What you find dere to care about[1]
I never understan';
It only dutty up you mout',
An' mek you less a man.

I see it throw you 'pon de grass
An' mek you want no food,
While people scorn you as dey pass
An' see you vomit blood.

De fust beginnin' of it all,
You stood up calm an' cool,
An' put you' back agains' de wall
An' cuss our teacher fool.[2]

You cuss me too de se'fsame day
Because a say you wrong,[3]
An' pawn you' books an' went away
Widout anedder song.[4]

Your parents' hearts within dem sink,
When to your yout'ful lip
Dey watch you raise de glass to drink,
An' shameless tek each sip.'

---

1. To like.
2. Abused our schoolmaster and called him a fool. To "cuss" is to "abuse" : to "cuss bad word" is to "swear."
3. Because I said you were wrong.
4. Without another word.

I see you in de dancing-booth,
But all your joy is vain,
For on your fresh an' glowin' youth
Is stamped dat ugly stain.

Dat ugly stain of drink, my frien',
Has cost you your best girl,
An' mek you fool 'mongst better men
When your brain's in a whirl.

You may smoke just a bit indeed,
I like de "white seal"[5] well;
Aldough I do not use de weed,
I'm fond o' de nice smell.

But wait until you're growin' old
An' gettin' weak an' bent,
An' feel your blood a-gettin' cold
'Fo' you tek stimulent.

Then it may mek you stronger feel
While on your livin' groun';[6]
But ole Time, creepin' on your heel,
Soon, soon will pull you down:

Soon, soon will pull you down, my frien',
De rum will help her[7] too;
An' you'll give way to better men,
De best dat you can do.[8]

---

5. The name of a brand of cigarettes.
6. While in this life.
7. Time.
8. Which is the best thing you can do.

Heart-Stirrings

You axe me as de bell begin fe 'trike,
Me Mikey, ef de wuk a didn' like;
De queshton, like de bell, soun' in me heart
Same how de anvil usual mek me 'tart.[1]

You's a chil'[2] an' know naught 'bout de wul' yet,
But you'll grow an' larn t'ings you won't feget;
You lub you' life, an' t'ink dere's nuttin' better,
Yet all you' pickny dream dem soon will 'ketter.[3]

Tek me advice ya, chil', an' as you grow
Don't choose a wuk dat you no like: aldough
You might see money in o' it, at lengt'
You will get tired o' it an' repent.

A suffer, but I t'ink it mek me wise;
It wasn' fe de money 'trike me yeyes,[4]
But "water mo' 'an flour"[5] is true wud,
An' eye-water run too long tu'n to blood.[6]

Hard life caan' kill me, but annoyance might,
Me lub me right, an' fe it me wi' fight:
Me wi' lef beef fe nyam an' choose cow-lung,
Fe sabe meself from an annoying tongue.[7]

But sometime', chil', you jump from fryin'-pan
'Traight in a fire; an', try as you can,
You caan' come out, but always wishin' den
Fe get back in de fryin'-pan again.

---

1. Just as the sound of an anvil—the speaker was a blacksmith—makes me start and arouses disagreeable recollections, so does your question.
2. Child.
3. Scatter.
4. It wasn't the attraction of the high wages.
5. "Beggars can't be choosers." The references is to dumplings made with too much water.
6. This means that he (the speaker) was unhappy at home.
7. Prov. Xv. 17; xvii. I.

Ole Buccra Dabis, libing easy life,
One night get mad an' kill himself an' wife;
Den we hear t'ings we neber be'n know yet,
De b'uccra man was ears an' han's in debt.

Miss Laura lean back in her rockin'-chair
So sweet dat we might jes' t'ink she no care
'Bout naught; yet some say dat 'cos she caan' get
Mas' Charley fe him husban'[8] she deh fret.

Dat's how life 'tan',[9] me chil"; dere is somet'ing
Deep down in we dat you can neber bring
People, howeber wise, fe understan':
Caan' feel man heart same how you feel dem han'.

Fe lub, me chil', lub wha' you natur' hate![10] —
You'll live in misery, prayin' hard fe fait',
Which won't come eben ef you 'crub you' knees
In fifty quart o' corn an' lady-peas.[11]

Fe hate a t'ing you whole min' come in one:
You try fe keep it[12] back much as you can,
But "flesh caan' conquer 'perit" Bible say,
You hab fe give it up,[13] an' den 'top pray.

Me carry hell, me chit', in a me ches',
Me laugh, me cry, me couldn' get no res';
Eat all de same an' neber fatter less[14]
Dan now, aldough me min' was so distress'.

---

8. Master Charley for her husband.
9. Stands = is.
10. If you try to make yourself love what your nature hates. This line is partly an exclamation, partly an interrogation.
11. Black-eye peas.
12. The hatred.
13. Give up trying.
14. Less fat.

An' though a feel it hard, a wouldn' fret;
Me min' don't mek so, but it eber set
Fe conquer, yet it couldn' wash away
De t'oughts dem dat come 'tronger ebery day.

You 'stan',[15] me chil'? I caan' explain it mo':
Life funny bad, so is de ways also;
For what we fink is right is often wrong,
We live in sorrow as we journey 'long.

---

15. Do you understand?

De Dog-Rose

Growin' by de corner-stone,[1]
    See de pretty flow'r-tree blows,
Sendin' from de prickly branch
    A lubly bunch o' red dog-rose.[2]

An' de bunch o' crimson red,
    Boastin' on de dark blue tree,
Meks it pretty, prettier yet
    Jes' as dat dog-rose can be.[3]

Young Miss Sal jes'[4] come from school:
    Freddy, fresh from groun' an' grub,
Pick de dog-rose off de tree,
    Gib Miss Sal to prove his lub.

Then I watch on as dem kiss
    Right aroun' de corner-stone,
An' my heart grow vex' fe see
    How dem foolish when alone.

An' I listen to deir talk,
    As dey say dey will be true;
"Eber true" I hear dem pledge,
    An' dat naught can part dem two.

De petchary[5] laugh an' jig,
    Sittin' on a bamboo low;
Seems him guess, jes' like mese'f
    How de whole t'ing gwin' fe go.

---

1. Angle of the house.
2. A dark red sweet-rose.
3. Makes it pretty—as pretty as it is possible for a dog-rose to be.
4. Just.
5. Grey king-bird.

Time gwon,[6] an' de rose is not:
    I see Fred, wi' eyes all dim,
Huggin' up de corner-stone,
    For his love has jilted him;

Left him for anedder man
    Wid a pile o' money,
Dat he carried from his land
    O' de Injin coney.[7]

Wonder whe' de petchary?
    De rose-tree is dead an' gone;
Sal sit in de big great-house,[8]
    Cooin' to her baby son.

---

6. Goes on; passes away.
7. England or Scotland, the home of the Indian coney (common rabbit)—pronounced *cunny*.
8. The principal house on a property is so called.

A Midnight Woman to the Bobby

No palm me up,[1] you dutty brute,
You' jam mout' mash[2] like ripe bread-fruit;
You fas'n now, but wait lee ya,[3]
I'll see you grunt under de law.

You t'ink you wise[4], but we wi' see;
You not de fus' one fas' wid me;
I'll lib fe see dem tu'n you out,
As sure as you got dat mash' mout'.

I born right do'n beneat' de clack[5]
(You ugly brute, you tu'n you' back?)
Don' t'ink dat I'm a come-aroun',[6]
I born right 'way in 'panish Town.

Care how you try, you caan' do mo'
Dan many dat was hyah befo';[7]
Yet whe' dey all o' dem te-day?[8]
De buccra dem no kick dem 'way?[9]

---

1. Don't put your hands on me.
2. Your d—d mouth is all awry.
3. You are fast (meddling, officious) now, but wait a little, d'you hear?
4. You think you're wise.
5. The clock on the public buildings at Spanish Town.
6. Day-labourers, men and women, in Kingston streets and wharves, famous for the heavy weights they carry, are called come-arounds.
7. No matter how you try, you can't do more than your predecessors (all that were here before.)
8. Yet where are they all today?
9. Did not the buccra (white man) kick them away (dismiss them?)

Ko[10] pon you' jam samplatta[11] nose:
'Cos you wear Mis'r Koshaw clo'es[12]
You fink say youts de only man,[13]
Yet fus' time[14] ko how you be'n 'tan'. [15]

You big an' ugly ole tu'n-foot[16]
Be'n neber know fe wear a boot;
An' chigger nyam you' tumpa toe,[17]
Till nit full i' like herrin' roe.

You come from mountain naked-'kin,[18]
An' Lard a mussy! you be'n thin,
For all de bread-fruit dem be'n done,
Bein' 'poil' up by de tearin' sun:[19]

De coco[20] couldn' bear at all,
For, Lard! de groun' was pure white~marl;
An' t'rough de rain part[21] o' de year
De mango tree dem couldn' bear.

An' when de pinch o' time you feel
A 'pur you a you' chigger heel,[22]
You lef you' district, big an' coarse,
An' come join'[23] buccra Police Force.

---

10. Look.
11. A piece of leather cut somewhat larger than the size of the foot, and tired sandal-wise to it: said of anything that is flat and broad.
12. Mr. Kershaw's clothes, *i.e.*, police uniform. Col. Kershaw, Inspector-General of Police in 1911 (when this poem was written) and for many years before.
13. A mighty fine fellow.
14. When I knew your first.
15. Look what sort of figure you cut.
16. Turned-in foot.
17. And chigoes (burrowing fleas) had eaten into your maimed toe, and nits (young chigoes) had filled it.
18. Naked skin, *i.e.*, with your shirt and trousers full of holes.
19. Having been spoilt by the hot sun. Pronounce "bein'" as a monosyllable.
20. An edible root (*Colocasia antiquorum*.)
21. During some months.
22. And when you felt hard times spurring you in your chigger-eaten heel.
23. Came and joined.

CLAUDE MCKAY

An' now you don't wait fe you' glass,[24]
But trouble me wid you' jam fas';[25]
But wait, me frien', you' day wi' come,
I'll see you go same lak a some.[26]

Say wha'?—'res' me?[27] —you go to hell!
You t'ink Judge don't know unno well?[28]
You t'ink him gwin' go sentance[29] me
Widout a soul fe witness i'?

---

24. You don't wait for the right and proper moment.
25. With all your infernal forwardness and officiousness.
26. Same like some = just as others before you did.
27. What's that?—arrest me?
28. D'you think the magistrate doesn't know your tricks? Unno or Onnoo is an African word, meaning "you" collectively.
29. Pronounce the *a* in 'ah,' but without accent.

Mother Dear

"Husban", I am goin'—
Though de brooklet is a-flowin',
An' de coolin' breeze is blowin'
    Softly by;
Hark, how strange de cow is mooin',
An' our Jennie's pigeons cooin',
While I feel de water[1] growin'
    Climbing high."

"Akee[2] trees are laden,
But de yellow leaves are fadin'
Like a young an' bloomin' maiden
    Fallen low;
In de pond de ducks are wadin'
While my body longs for Eden,[3]
An' my weary breat is gledin'
    'Way from you.

"See dem John-crows[4] flyin'!
'Tis a sign dat I am dyin';
Oh, I'm wishful to be lyin'
    All alone:
Fait'ful husban', don't go cryin',
Life is one long self-denyin'
All-surrenderin' an' sighin'
    Livin' moan."

"Wife, de parson's prayin',
Won't you listen what he's sayin',
Spend de endin' of your day in
    Christ our Lord?"

---

1. The water of dropsy rising from the legs towards the heart.
2. *Cupania sapida*, bearing beautiful red fruits.
3. To English readers this and the next (gledin'=gliding) would hardly seem to be rhymes. Nevertheless they are so.
4. Turkey-buzzards.

CLAUDE MCKAY

But de sound of horses neighin',
Baain' goats an' donkeys brayin',
Twitt'rin' birds an' children playin'
    Was all she heard.

Things she had been rearin',
Only those could claim her hearin',
When de end we had been fearin'
    Now had come:
Now her last pain she is bearin',
Now de final scene is nearin',
An' her vacant eyes are starin'
    On her home.[5]

Oh! it was heart-rendin'
As we watched de loved life endin',
Dat sweet sainted spirit bendin'
    To de death:
Gone all further hope of mendin',
With de angel Death attendin',
An' his slayin' spirit blendin'
    With her breath.

---

5. The spot in the garden she had chosen for her burial place.

KITE-FLYING

Higher fly, my pretty kite,
    Over distant towers;
Paper-made, red, blue an' white,
    All my fav'rite colours.[1]

As up an' up an' up you mount
    On your way to heaven, Thoughts
come, which I cannot count,
    Of the times I've striven

Just to soar away like you,
    Rising to a happier sphere
Deep within yon skies of blue,
    Far from all de strife an' care.

You have got you' singer[2] on,
    Let me hear your singing,
Hear you' pleasant bee-like tone
    On de breezes ringing.

Wider dash your streamin' tail,
    Keep it still a-dancin'!
As across de ditch you sail,
    By the tree-tops glancin'.

Messengers[3] I send along,
    Lee round papers of bright red;
Up they go to swell you' song,
    Climbin' on the slimber[4] t'read.

---

1. The *l* is swallowed, and the rhyme is good.
2. A strip of paper shaped like a half moon, and stretched on a thread running from one top corner of the kite to the other.
3. Round slips of paper, which go twirling up the kite-string.
4. Slender.

Higher fiy, my pretty kite,
    Higher, ever higher;
Draw me with you to your height
    Out the earthly mire.

IONE

Say if you lub me, do tell me truly,
    Ione, Ione;
For, O me dearie, not'in' can part we,
    Ione, Ione.

Under de bamboo, where de fox-tail[1] grew,
    Ione, Ione.
While do cool breeze blew—sweet, I did pledge
  you,
    Ione, Ione.

Where calalu[2] grows, an' yonder book flows,
    Ione, Ione.
I held a dog-rose under your li'l[3] nose,
    Ione, Ione.

There where de lee stream plays wid de sunbeam
    Ione, Ione.
True be'n de love-gleam as a sweet day-dream,
    Ione, Ione.

Watchin' de bucktoe[4] under de shadow
    Ione, Ione.
Of a pear-tree low dat in de stream grow,
    Ione, Ione.

Mek me t'ink how when we were lee children,
    Ione, Ione.
We used to fishen[5] in old Carew Pen[6],
    Ione, Ione.

---

1. A grass with heavy plumes.
2. Spinach, but not the English kind.
3. Little.
4. Small crawfish.
5. Fish.
6. The Jamaican equivalent for ranche.

CLAUDE MCKAY

Like tiny meshes, curl your black tresses,
        Ione, Ione.
An' my caresses tek widout blushes,
        Ione, Ione.

Kiss me, my airy winsome lee fairy,
        Ione, Ione.
Are you now weary, little canary,
        Ione, Ione.

Then we will go, pet, as it is sunset,
        Ione, Ione.
Tek dis sweet vi'let, we will be one yet,
        Ione, Ione.

KILLIN' NANNY

Two little pickny is watchin',
    While a goat is led to deat';
Dey are little ones of two years,
    An' know naught of badness yet.

De goat is bawlin' fe mussy,[1]
    An' de children watch de sight
As de butcher re'ch[2] his sharp knife,
    An' 'tab[3] wid all his might.

Dey see de red blood flowin';
    An' one chil' trimble an' hide
His face in de mudder's bosom,
    While t'udder look on wide-eyed.

De tears is fallin' down hotly
    From him on de mudder's knee;
De udder wid joy is starin',
    An' clappin' his han's wid glee.

When dey had forgotten Nanny,
    Grown men I see dem again;
An' de forehead of de laugher
    Was brand[4] wid de mark of Cain.

---

1. Mercy.
2. Reaches, lays hold of.
3. Stabs.
4. Branded.

My Native Land, My Home

Dere is no land dat can compare
    Wid you where'er I roam;
In all de wul' none like you fair,
    My native land, my home.

Jamaica is de nigger's place,
    No mind whe' some declare;
Although dem call we "no-land race,"
    I know we home is here.

You give me life an' nourishment,
    No udder land I know;
My lub I neber can repent,
    For all to you l owe.

E'en ef you mek me beggar die,
    I'll trust you all de same,
An' none de less on you rely,
    Nor saddle you wid blame.

Though you may cas'[1] me from your breas'
    An' trample me to deat',
My heart will trus' you none de less,
    My land I won't feget.

An' I hope none o' your sons would
    Refuse deir strengt' to lend,
An' drain de last drop o' deir blood
    Their country to defend.

You draw de t'ousan' from deir shore,
    An' all 'long keep dem please';[2]
De invalid come here fe cure,
    You heal all deir disease.

---

1. Cast.
2. And keep them amused and happy all along (all the time of their stay.)

Your fertile soil grow all o 't'ings[3]
    To full de naygur's wants,
'Tis seamed wid neber-failing springs[4]
    To give dew to de plants.[5]

You hab all t'ings fe mek life bles',
    But buccra 'pail de whole
Wid gove'mint[6] an' all de res',
    Fe worry naygur soul.

Still all dem little chupidness[7]
    Caan' tek away me lub;
De time when I'll tu'n 'gains' you is
    When you can't give me grub.

---

3. All of (the) things.
4. Brooks.
5. The dew falls heavily in the valley-bottoms.
6. Government.
7. Those little stupidnesses.

Two-An'-Six

Merry voices chatterin',
Nimble feet dem patterin',
Big an' little, faces gay,
Happy day dis market day.

Sateday![1] de marnin' break,
Soon, soon market-people wake;
An' de light shine from de moon
While dem boy, wid pantaloon
Roll up ober dem knee-pan,
'Tep[2] across de buccra lan'
To de pastur whe' de harse[3]
Feed along wid de jackass,
An' de mule cant' in de track[4]
Wid him tail up in him back,
All de ketchin' to defy,
No ca' how[5] dem boy might try.

In de early marnin' -tide,
When de cocks crow on de hill
An' de stars are shinin' still,
Mirrie by de fireside
Hots[6] de coffee for de lads
Comin' ridin' on de pads
T'rown across dem animul—
Donkey, harse too, an' de mule,
Which at last had come do'n cool.[7]
On de bit dem hol' dem full:

---

1. Saturday.
2. Step.
3. Where the horse.
4. Canters in the track. A Jamacian pasture is seamed with tracks made by the animals in walking.
5. I don't care how; no matter how.
6. Warms.
7. Given up his skittishness.

Racin' ober pastur' lan',
See dem comin' ebery man,
Comin' fe de steamin' tea[8]
Ober hilly track an' lea.

Hard-wuk'd donkey on de road
Trottin' wid him ushal[9] load,—
Hamper[10] pack' wi' yarn an' grain,
Sour-sop,[11] an' Gub'nor cane.[12]

Cous' Sun[13] sits in hired dray,
Drivin' 'long de market way j
Whole week grindin' sugar-cane
T'rough de boilin' sun an' rain,
Now, a'ter[14] de toilin' hard,
He goes seekin' his reward,
While he's thinkin' in him min'
Of de dear ones Ief' behin',
Of de loved though ailin' wife,
Darlin' treasure of his life,
An' de picknies, six in all,
Whose 'nuff[15] burdens 'pon him fall:

Seben[16] lovin' ones in need,
Seben hungry mouths fe feed;
On deir wants he thinks alone,
Neber dreamin' of his own,
But gwin' on wid joyful face
Till him re'ch[17] de market-place.

---

8. Generic name for any non-alcoholic hot drink.
9. Usual, pronounced without the second *u*.
10. Panniers.
11. *Anona muricata*—a fruit.
12. Governor cane; a yellow-striped sugar-cane.
13. Cousin James. Sun is the regular nickname for James.
14. After.
15. Enough = many.
16. Seven.
17. Till he reaches.

CLAUDE MCKAY

Sugar bears no price te-day,
Though it is de mont' o' May,
When de time is hellish hot,
An' de water-cocoanut[18]
An' de cane bebridge[19] is nice,
Mix' up wid a lilly ice.[20]
Big an' little, great an' small,
Afou yam is all de call;[21]
Sugar tup an' gill[22] a quart,
Yet de people hab de heart
Wantin' brater[23] top o' i',
Want de sweatin' higgler fe
Ram de pan an' pile i' up,
Yet sell i' fe so-so tup.[24]

Cousin Sun is lookin' sad,
As de market is so bad;
'Pon him han' him res' him chin,
Quietly sit do'o thinkin'
Of de loved wife sick in bed,
An' de children to be fed—
What de labourers would say
When dem know him couldn' pay;
Also what about de mill
Whe' him hire[25] from ole Bill;
So him think, an' think on so,
Till him t'oughts no more could go.

Then he got up an' began
Pickin' up him sugar-pan:[26]
In his ears rang t'rough de din

---

18. Immature cocoanut, the milk of which is a delicious drink.
19. Beverage.
20. Mixed up with a little ice.
21. The variety of yam called "ahfoo" is the thing principally asked for by young and old.
22. Tup (twopence of the old Jamaica coinage) is 1 ½d: gill, ¾d. So "tup and gill" is 2 ¼d.
23. Insist on having *brahter*, a little extra on top of (over) the quart.
24. Sell it for a bare tup.
25. Which he hires, or hired.
26. His sugar pans (tins.)

"Only two-an'-six a tin!"
What a tale he'd got to tell,
How bad, bad de sugar sell!

Tekin' out de lee amount,
Him set do'n an' begin count;
All de time him min' deh doubt[27]
How expenses would pay out;
Ah, it gnawed him like de ticks,
Sugar sell fe two-an'-six!

So he journeys on de way,
Feelin' sad dis market day;
No e'en buy[28] a little cake
To gi'e baby when she wake,—
Passin' 'long de candy-shop
'Douten eben mek a stop
To buy drops fe las'y[29] son,
For de lilly cash nea' done.
So him re'ch him own a groun',
An' de children scamper roun',
Each one stretchin' out him han',
Lookin' to de poor sad man.

Oh, how much he felt de blow,
As he watched dem face fall low,
When dem wait an' nuttin' came
An' drew back deir han's wid shame!
But de sick wife kissed his brow:
"Sun, don't get down-hearted now;
Ef we only pay expense
We mus' wuk we common-sense,
Cut an' carve, an' carve an' cut,
Mek gill sarbe fe quattiewut';[30]
We mus' try mek two ends meet

---

27. His mind is doubting.
28. Doesn't even buy.
29. Lasty (lahsty,) pet name for the Benjamin of a family.
30. Make ¾d. serve for quattieworth, 1 ½d.

CLAUDE MCKAY

Neber mind how hard be it.
We won't mind de haul an' pull,
While dem pickny belly full."[31]

An' de shadow lef' him face,
An' him felt an inward peace,
As he blessed his better part
For her sweet an' gentle heart:
"Dear one o' my heart, my breat',
Won't I lub you to de deat'?
When my heart is weak an' sad,
Who but you can mek it glad?"

So dey kissed an' kissed again,
An' deir t'oughts were not on pain,
But was 'way down in de sout'
Where dey'd wedded in deir yout',

In de marnin' of deir life
Free from all de grief an' strife,
Happy in de marnin' light,
Never thinkin' of de night.

So dey k'lated[32] eberyt'ing;
An' de profit it could bring,
A'ter all de business fix',[33]
Was a princely two-an'-six.

---

31. If only the children have enough to eat.
32. Calculated.
33. After all the business was fixed, *i.e.*, when the accounts were made up.

Compensation

Dere is a rest-place for de weary feet,
An' for de bitter cup a conquering sweet:
For sore an' burdened hearts dere'll be a balm,
And after days of tempest comes a calm.

For every smallest wrong dere is a right,
An' t'rough de dark shall gleam a ray of light:
Oppression for a season may endure,
But 'tis true wud, "For ebery ill a cure."

Den let me not t'ink hard of those who use
Deir power tyrannously an' abuse:
Let me remember always while I live,
De noblest of all deeds is to forgive.

This, not revenge, is sweet: this lif's[1] de soul
An' meks it wort' while[2] in a empty wul':
Far better than an old an' outworn creed
'Tis each day to do one such noble deed.

---

1. Lifts.
2. Something worth.

HEARTLESS RHODA

Kiss me, as you want it so;
    Lub me, ef it wort' de while;[1]
Yet I feel it an' I know[2]
Dat, as t'rough de wul' you go,
    You will oft look back an' smile
At de t'ings which you now do.

Tek me to de church te-day,
    Call me wife as you go home;
Hard fate, smilin' at us, say[3]
Dat de whole is so-so play;
    Soon de ushal en' will come,
An' we both will choice[4] our way.

        * * * *

Spare you' breat', me husban' true,
    I be'n marry you fe fun:[5]
Lub dat las' long is a few,[6]
An' I hadn' much fe you.
    I be'n tell you it would done,[7]
All whe' come is wha' you do. [8]
Life I only care to see
    In de way dat udders[9] live;
I experiment to be

---

1. Love me, if it is worth while, *i.e.*, if you think it is worth while.
2. Yet I feel and know.
3. Says.
4. Choose, *i.e.*, go our several ways.
5. I married you with no serious purpose.
6. Seldom met with.
7. I did tell (told) you it would soon come to an end.
8. All that has happened is your doing.
9. Others.

All dat fate can mek o' me:
    Glad I tek all whe' she give,
For I'm hopin' to be free.[10]

---

10. A free paraphrase will best explain the meaning of these six lines. Rhoda sees other girls marry, and out of pure curiosity she wants to find out what married life is like. So she makes the experiment,—though this (marriage) is only one of the things that Fate has in store for her. And she takes gladly whatever Fate gives, always hoping (and meaning) to change the present experience for another.

CLAUDE MCKAY

A Dream

The roosters give the signal for daybreak,
    And through my window[1] pours the grey of
        morn;
Refreshing breezes fan me as I wake,
    And down the valley sounds the wesly[2] horn.

Day broadens, and I ope the window wide,[3]
    And brilliant sunbeams, mixing, rush between
The gaping blinds, while down at my bedside
    I kneel to utter praise to the Unseen.

The torch-light glistens through the wattle-pane,[4]
    And clouds of smoke wreathe upward to the
        skies;
My brother at the squeezer juices cane,[5]
    And visions of tea-hour before me rise.

Leaving the valley's cup the fleeting fog
    Steals up the hill-sides decked with sunbeams
        rare,
Which send their search-rays 'neath the time-worn
        log,
    And drive the sleeping majoes[6] from their lair.

But there are some that yest'reve was the last
    For them to sleep into their watery bed;
For now my treacherous fish-pot has them fast,
    Their cruel foe which they had so long dread'.[7]

---

1. The window is a jalousie, and its blinds (slats) are shut.
2. Word of uncertain origin. The wesly horn sounds when any work in common is to be undertaken.
3. Throw the slats into a horizontal position.
4. The bedroom is separated from the kitchen by panes of undaubed wattle, through which is seen the glimmer of the burning torch-wood.
5. At the squeezer (a rough home-made machine) is extracting juice from sugar-canes.
6. Pronounce the *ma* in French—fresh-water shrimps, which live in the hill-side brooklets.
7. Whom for so long a time they had dreaded.

Right joyfully I hear the school-bell ring,
    And by my sister's side away I trot;
I'm happy as the swee-swees[8] on the wing,
    And feel naught but contentment in my lot.

I lightly gambol on the school-yard green,
    And where the damsels[9] by the bamboo grove
In beautiful and stately growth are seen,
    For tiny shiny star-apples I rove.

* * * * * *

The morning wind blows softly past my door,
    And we prepare for work with gladsome heart;
Sweetly the wesly horn resounds once more,
    A warning that 'tis time for us to start.

I scamper quickly 'cross the fire-burnt soil,
    And the coarse grass-tufts prick my tender feet;
I watch my father at his honest toil,
    And wonder how he stands the sun's fierce heat.

A winding footpath down the woodland leads,
    And through the tall fox-tails I wend my way
Down to the brooklet where the pea-dove feeds,
    And bucktoes[10] in the water are at play.

And watching as the bubbles rise and fall,
    I hear above the murmur of the dale
The tropic music dear to great and small,
    The joyous outburst of the nightingale.

• • • • • •

Gone now those happy days when all was blest,
    For I have left my home and kindred dear;
In a strange place I am a stranger's guest,
    The pains, the real in life, I've now to bear.

---

8. Quits. The name imitates their chirping song.
9. The damsel (corruption of damson, probably) is like a small star-apple.
10. Small crawfish.

No more again I'll idle at my will,
    Running the mongoose down upon the lea;
No more I'll jostle[11] Monty up the hill,
    To pick the cashews[12] off the laden tree.

I feel the sweetness of those days again,
    And hate, so hate, on the past scenes to look;
All night in dreaming comes the awful pain,
    All day I groan beneath the iron yoke.

In mercy then, ye Gods, deal me swift death!
    Ah! you refuse, and life instead you give;
You keep me here and still prolong my breath,
    That I may suffer all the days I live.

* * * *

'Tis home again, but not the home of yore;
    Sadly the scenes of bygone days I view,
And as I walk the olden paths once more,
    My heart grows chilly as the morning dew.

But see I today again my life is glad,
    My heart no more is lone, nor will it pine;
A comfort comes, an earthly fairy clad
    In white, who guides me with her hand in mine.

Her lustrous eyes gleam only tender love,
    And viewing her, an angel form I see;
I feed my spirit on my gentle dove,
    My sweetheart Lee, my darling Idalee.[13]

And where the peenies glow with greenish fire,
    We kiss and kiss and pledge our hearts as true
Of sweet love-words and hugs we never tire,
    But felt more sorry that they were so few.

• • • • •

---

11. Race and foul.
12. A fruit (*Anacardium occidentale*.)
13. This tacking of a syllable on to well-known names is common in Jamaica.

I leave my home again, wand'ring afar,
　　But goes with me her true, her gentle heart,
Ever to be my hope, my guiding star,
　　And whisperings of comfort to impart.

Methinks we're strolling by the woodland stream,
　　And my frame thrills with joy to hear her sing:
But, O my God! 'tis all—'tis all a dream;
　　This is the end, the rude awakening.

Rise and Fall

(Thoughts of Burns—with apologies to his immortal spirit for making him speak in Jamaican dialect.)

Dey read[1] 'em again an' again,
    An' laugh an' cry[2] at 'em in turn;
I felt I was gettin' quite vain,
    But dere was a lesson fe learn.

My poverty quickly took wing,
    Of life no experience had I;
I couldn' then want anyt'ing
    Dat kindness or money could buy.

Dey tek me away from me lan',
    De gay o' de wul' to behold,
An' roam me t'rough palaces gran',
    An' show'red on me honour untold.

I went to de ballroom at night,
    An' danced wid de belles of de hour;
Half dazed by de glitterin' light,
    I lounged in de palm-covered bower.

I flirted wid beautiful girls,
    An' drank o' de wine flowin' red;
I felt my brain movin' in whirls,
    An' knew I was losin' my head.

But soon I was tired of it all,
    My spirit was weary to roam;[3]
De life grew as bitter as gall,
    I hungered again for my home.

---

1. Preterite.
2. Laughed and cried.
3. Sick of roaming.

Te-day I am back in me lan',
    Forgotten by all de gay throng,
A poorer but far wiser man,
    An' knowin' de right from de wrong.

Beneath the Yampy[1] Shade

We sit beneat' de yampy shade,
    My lee sweetheart an' I;
De gully[2] ripples 'cross de glade,
    Tom Rafflins[3] hurry by.

Her pa an' ma about de fiel'
    Are brukin'[4] sugar-pine;
An' plenty, plenty is de yiel',
    Dem look so pink[5] an' fine.

We listen to a rapturous chune[6]
    Outpourin' from above;
De swee-swees[7], blithesome birds of June,
    They sing to us of love.

She plays wid de triangle leaves,
    Her hand within mine slips;
She murmurs love, her bosom heaves,
    I kiss her ripe, ripe lips.

De cockstones[8] raise deir droopin' heads
    To view her pretty feet;
De skellions[9] trimble in deir beds,
    Dey grudge our lub so sweet—

---

1. The Yampy, or Indian Yam, has very beautiful triangular leaves. Yams of all kinds climb, like hops, on sticks or trees.
2. Brook. The word is more generally used in the sense of *precipice*.
3. Mad ants, which run very quickly.
4. Breaking. Pine-apples are gathered by bending down the stalk, which snaps clearly off.
5. Choice, nice. *Cf.* the phrase, Pink of perfection.
6. Tune.
7. Quits.
8. Red peas, French beans.
9. Scallions—a non-bulbing onion.

Love sweeter than a bridal dream,
    A mudder's fondest kiss
Love purer than a crystal stream,
    De height of eart'ly bliss.

We hear again de swee-swees' song
    Outpourin' on de air;
Dey sing for yout', an' we are young
    An' know naught 'bouten care.

We sit beneat' de yampy shade,
    We pledge our hearts anew;
De swee-swees droop, de bell-flowers[10] fade
    Before our love so true.

---

10. *Datura suaveolens*, whose great white trumpets flag as the sun gets hot.

To Inspector W.E. Clark

(On the Eve of His Departure for England)

Farewell, dear Sir, a sad farewell!
An' as across the deep you sail,
    Bon voyage we wish you:
We love you deepest as we can,[1]
As officer an' gentleman,
    With love sIncere an' true.

Though often you have been our judge,
We never owed you one lee grudge,
    For you were always fair:
So, as the sad farewell we say,
May Neptune guide you, Sir, we pray,
    With ever watchful care.

But as you travel to our home,[2]
Sad are the strange thoughts which *will* come,
    Bringin' an aching pain;
That as this is a fitful life,
With disappointments ever rife,
    We may not meet again.

Yet while our hearts are filled with grief,
The god of hope brings sweet relief
    An' bids us not despair:
Of all our thoughts we cannot tell,
But wish you, Sir, a fond farewell,
    A farewell of good cheer.

21st *May*, 1911

---

1. With all our heart.
2. England.

To Clarendon Hills and H.A.H.

Loved Clarendon hills,
Dear Clarendon hills,
Oh! I feel de chills,
Yes, I feel de chills
Coursin' t'rough me frame
When I call your name,[1]
Dear Clarendon hills,
Loved Clarendon hills.

Wand'rin', wand'rin' far,
Weary, wan'drin' far
'Douten guidin' star,
Not a guidin' star,
Still my love's for you
Ever, ever true,
Though I wander far,
Weary wander far.

H. A. H., my frien',
Ever cherished frien',
I'll return again,
Yes, return again:
Think, O think of me
Tossed on life's dark sea,
H. A. H., my frien',
Dearest, fondest frien'.

Ah, dear frien' o' mine,
Love me, frien' o' mine,
Wid that love of thine
Passin' love of womenkin',[2]
More dan love of womenkin':
Clasp me to your breast,

---

1. Speak of you.
2. 2 Sam. i. 26.

Pillow me to rest,
Fait'ful frien' o' mine,
Truest frien' o' mine.

Though you may be sad,
Sorrowin' an' sad,
Never min' dat, lad,
Don't you min' dat, lad!
Live, O live your life,
Trample on de strife,
Though you may be sad,
Always, always sad.

Loved Clarendon hills,
Cherished frien' o' mine,
Oh, my bosom thrills,
Soul an' body pine:
Trough de wul' I rove,
Pinin' for your love,
Blest Clarendon hills,
Dearest frien' o' mine.

When You Want a Bellyful

When you want a bellyful,
    Tearin' piece o' one,[1]
Mek up fire, wash you' pot,
    Full i' wid cockstone.

Nuttin' good as cockstone soup
    For a bellyful;
Only, when you use i' hot,
    You can sweat no bull.[2]

An' to mek you know de trut',
    Dere's anedder flaw;
Ef you use too much o' i',
    It wi' paunch you' maw.[3]

Growin' wid de fat blue corn,
    Pretty cockstone peas—
Lilly blossom, vi'let-like,[4]
    Drawin' wuker bees—

We look on dem growin' dere,
    Pokin' up dem head,
Lilly, lilly, t'rough de corn,
    Till de pod dem shed.[5]

An' we watch de all-green pods
    Stripin' bit by bit;
Green leaves gettin' yellow coat,
    Showin dey were fit.[6]

---

1. This whole line is a single intensifying adjective; and the two lines together are equivalent to "When you want a tremendous bellyful."
2. It makes you sweat like a ('no'—pronounced very short in this sense) bull.
3. Make your belly swell.
4. Violet coloured.
5. Until the pools are formed.
6. Showing that the peas were fit to pick.

So we went an' pull dem up,[7]
    Reaped a goodly lot,
Shell some o' de pinkish grain,
    Put dem in a pot.[8]

But I tell you, Sir, again,
    Cockstone soup no good;[9]
From experience I fink
    'Tis de wus' o' food.[10]

When de reapin'-time come roun',
    I dry fe me part;[11]
Sellin i', when it get scarce,
    For a bob a quart.[12]

When you need a bellyful,
    Grip! n' piece o' one,
Shub up fire under pot,
    Put in dry cockstone.

---

7. These red peas are pulled up by the roots.
8. In the pot.
9. Is not good.
10. The worst of the food.
11. I dry my share.
12. The usual price is 'bit' *i.e.*, 4 ½ d.

Strokes of the Tamarind Switch

I Dared not look at him,
My eyes with tears were dim,
    My spirit filled with hate
        Of man's depravity,
    I hurried through the gate.

I went but I returned,
While in my bosom burned
    The monstrous wrong that we
        Oft bring upon ourselves,
    And yet we cannot see.

Poor little erring wretch!
The cutting tamarind switch
    Had left its bloody mark,
        And on his legs were streaks
    That looked like boiling bark.[1]

I spoke to him the while:
At first he tried to smile,
    But the long pent-up tears
        Came gushing-in a flood;
    He was but of tender years.

With eyes bloodshot and red,
He told me of a father dead
    And lads like himself rude,
        Who goaded him to wrong:
    He for the future promised to be good.

The mother yesterday
Said she was sending him away,
    Away across the seas:
        She told of futile prayers
    Said on her wearied knees.

---

1. Floors are dyed with a blood-red decoction made from the bark of trees

CLAUDE MCKAY

I wished the lad good-bye,
And left him with a sigh:
    Again I heard him talk—
        His limbs, he said, were sore.
    He could not walk.

I 'member when a smaller boy,
A mother's pride, a mother's joy,
    I too was very rude:
        They beat me too, though not the same,[2]
    And has it done me good?

NOTE BY THE AUTHOR: This was a lad of fifteen. No doubt he deserved the flogging administered by order of the Court: still, I could not bear to see him—my own flesh—stretched out over the bench, so I went away to the Post Office near by. When I returned, all was over. I saw his naked bleeding form, and through the terrible ordeal—so they told me—he never cried. But when I spoke to him he broke down, told me between his bursts of tears how he had been led astray by bad companions, and that his mother intended sending him over-sea. He could scarcely walk, so I gave him tickets for the tram. He had a trustful face. A few minutes after, my bitterness of spirit at the miserable necessity of such punishment came forth in song, which I leave rugged and unpolished as I wrote it at the moment.

---

2. Not so severely.

My Pretty Dan

I have a póliceman down at de Bay,[1]
An' he is true to me though far away.

I love my pólice, and he loves me too, ·
An' he has promised he'll be ever true.

My little bobby is a darlin' one,
An' he's de prettiest you could set eyes 'pon.

When he be'n station' up de countryside,
Fus' time I shun him sake o' foolish pride.

But as I watched him patrolling his beat,
I got to find out he was nice an' neat.

More still I foun' out he was extra kin',
An' dat his precious heart was wholly mine.

Den I became his own a true sweetheart,
An' while life last we're hopin' not fe part.

He wears a truncheon an' a handcuff case,
An' pretty cap to match his pretty face.

Dear lilly p'liceman stationed down de sout',
I feel your kisses rainin' on my mout'.

I could not give against[2] a policeman;
For if I do, how could I lub my Dan?

---

1. Morant Bay and similarly named seaside towns are always called simply, 'the Bay' by the people of the district.
2. Revile, abuse, vilify.

Prettiest of naygur is my dear police,
We'll lub foreber, an' our lub won't cease.

I have a policeman down at de Bay,
An' he is true to me though far away.

Ribber Come-Do'n[1]

From de top o' Clarendon hill
  Chock down to Clarendon plain
De ribber is rushin' an' tearin'
  'Count o' de showers o' rain.

An' a mudder, anxious an' sad,
  Two whole days be'n gone away,
A-buyin' fresh fish fe tu'n han'[2]
  Slap do'n at Old Harbour Bay.

But de dark ribber kept her back,
  Dat night she couldn' get home,
While a six-week-old baby wailed,
  An' wailed for a mudder to come.

An' a fader too was away
  'Cross de Minha[3] wukin' him groun',[4]
So him couldn' get home dat night
  Sake o' de ribber come-do'n.

Dere were four udder little ones
  'Sides de babe of six weeks old,
An' dey cried an' looked to no use,[5]
  An' oh dey were hungry an' cold!

So de lee fourteen-year-old gal,
  De eldest one o' de lot,
Was sad as she knelt by the babe
  An' byaed[6] her on de cot.

---

1. The river in flood.
2. To peddle.
3. The Rio Minho: pronounce 'miner.'
4. Cultivating his ground or provision-field.
5. In vain.
6. A verb formed from hushaby.

"Bya, bya, me baby,
    Baby want go sleepy."

She look 'pan de Manchinic[7] tree,
    Not a piece of mancha fe eat;
De Jack-fruit dem bear well anuff,
    But dere wasn't one o' dem fit.[8]

Nor puppa nor mumma could come,
    Aldough it be'n now nightfall;
De rain pour do'n an' de wind blow,
    An' de picknanies dem still bawl.
So de poo' Milly 'tarted out
    To whe' a kin' neighbour lib,
Fe see ef a bite o' nenyam[9]
    Dem couldn' p'raps manage fe gib.

"Ebenin', cousin Anna,
    Me deh beg you couple banna[10],
For dem tarra one[11] is berry hungry home;
    We puppa ober May,[12] ma,
    We mumma gone a Bay, ma,
An' we caan' tell warra'[13] time dem gwin' go
    come."

The kind district mother thought
    Of her own boy far away,
An' wondered much how he fared
    In a foreign land that day.

7. Martinique, the best variety of Banana.
8. Ripe.
9. Food.
10. I am begging a few bananas of you.
11. Those other ones, *i.e.*, the little children at home.
12. Over at Mayfield.
13. What.

She opened de cupboard door
　　An' took from it warra be'n sabe,
A few bits o' yam an' lee meal,
　　An' a pint o' milk fe de babe.

De parents dat night couldn' come,
　　De howlin' wind didn' lull,
But de picknanies went to bed
　　Wid a nuff nuff bellyful.

A Country Girl

"Lelia gal, why in this town do you stay?
Why, tell me, why did you wander away?
Why will you aimlessly foolishly roam,
Won't you come back to your old country home?"

"Country life, Fed, has no pleasures for me,
I wanted de gay o' de city to see,
To wear ebery Sunday a prettier gown,
Da's why I came to de beautiful town."

"Well, have you gotten de joys dat you sought?
If so, were not all o' dem too dearly bought?
Yes, Liel, you do wear a prettier dress,
But have you not suffered, my girl, more or less?

"Hold up your head! look not down, tell me truth,
Have you not bartered your innocent youth?
Are you de Lelia, true Lelia, of old,
Or have you swopped out your honour for gold?"

"Fed, it was horrid de lone country life!
I suffered-for sometimes e'en hunger was rife;
An' when I came, Fed, to try my chance here,
I thought there would be no more troubles to bear.

"But troubles there were an' in plenty, my lad,
Oh, dey were bitter, an' oh, I was sad!
Weary an' baffled an' hungry an' lone,
I gave up my spirit to sigh an' to moan.

"After dat?—O, Feddy, press me not so:
De truth ?—well, I sank to de lowest of de low;
I gave up all honour, I took a new name
An' tried to be happy, deep sunk in de shame.

"Dere was no other way, Fed, I could live,
Dat was de gift dat a gay town could give;
I tried to be glad in de open daylight,
But sorrowed an' moaned in de deep o' de night.

"No, Fed, I never could go home again:
'Worse than I left it?' ah, there was de pain,
To meet up wid some o' my former schoolmates
An' listen to all o' deir taunts an' deir hates.

"Dere now, you bound me to tell you o' all,
Of all de sad suff'rings dat led to my fall;
I'm gone past reclaiming, so what must I do
But live de bad life an' mek de good go?"

"Lelia, I want you to come out de sin,
Come home an' try a new life fe begin;
Mek up you min', gal, fe wuk wid you' han',
Plant peas an' corn in de fat country lan'.

"Dere is no life, gal, so pleasant, so good,
Contented and happy you'll eat your lee food;
No one at home know 'bout wha' you've jes' said,
So, Liel, of exposure you needn't be 'fraid."

"Don't t'ink I care 'bout exposure, my boy!
Dat which you call sin is now fe me joy;
Country for Lelia will have no more charm,
I'll live on de same way, 'twill do me no harm.

"And after all, many gals richer than me,
Pretty white girlies of better degree,
Live as I do, an' are happy an' gay,
Then why should not I be as happy as they?"

My Soldier-Lad

See yonder soldier-lad
In Zouave jacket clad?
   His lovin' heart is mine,
His heart so bright an' glad;
   My soul an' spirit combine
To love my soldier-lad.

   O my dear lilly soldier-lad,
      I am true an' so are you;
    And oh, my lovin' heart is glad,
      For I know that you are true.

My pretty soldier-boy,
He is my only joy:
   He loves me with his might,
A love without alloy,
   My one, my true delight,
My pretty soldier-boy.

   O my dear lilly soldier-lad, etc.

My own lee soldier true,
He is a bandsman too;
   An' when he's in the stand,
His sweet eyes playin' blue,
   He carries off the band,
My handsome soldier true.

   O my dear lilly soldier-lad, etc.

My precious lilly pet,
He plays a clarinet:
   De gals dem envy me,
But him they cannot get;
   Dem hate we both to see,
Me an' my precious pet.

O my dear lilly soldier-lad, etc.

Where coolin' breezes blow,
An' silvery gullies flow
    Do'n t'rough de bamboo grove,
The amorous pea-doves coo:
    They're cooin' of my love,
While freshenin' breezes blow.

O my dear lilly soldier-lad, etc.

My dear Bermudan lad
In baggy trousies clad,
    I love you wid whole heart,
A heart that's true an' glad;
    Our love can never part,
My darlin' bandsy lad.
O my dear lilly soldier-lad, etc.

My Mountain Home

De mango tree in yellow bloom,
 De pretty akee seed,
De mammee where de John-to-whits[1] come
 To have their daily feed,

Show you de place where I was born,
 Of which I am so proud,
'Mongst de banana-field an' corn
 On a lone mountain-road.

One Sunday marnin' 'fo' de hour
 Fe service-time come on,
Ma say dat I be'n born to her
 Her little las'y[2] son.

Those early days be'n neber dull,
 My heart was ebergreen;
How I did lub my little wul'
 Surrounded by pingwin![3]

An' growin' up, with sweet freedom
 About de yard I'd run;
An' tired out I'd hide me from
 De fierce heat of de sun.

So glad I was de fus' day when
 Ma sent me to de spring;
I was so happy feelin' then
 Dat I could do somet'ing.

---

1. Pronounce in two syllables.
2. Lasty, diminutive of "last."
3. The wild pineapple (*Bromelia Pinguin*.)

De early days pass quickly 'long,
    Soon I became a man,
An' one day found myself among
    Strange folks in a strange lan'.

My little joys, my wholesome min',
    Dey bullied out o' me,
And made me daily mourn an' pine
    An' wish dat I was free.

Dey taught me to distrust my life,
    Dey taught me what was grief;
For months I travailed in de strife,
    'Fa' I could find relief.

But I'll return again, my Will,
    An' where my wild ferns grow
An' weep for me on Dawkin's Hill,
    Dere, Willie, I shall go.

An' dere is somet'ing near forgot,
    Although I lub it best;
It is de loved, de hallowed spot
    Where my dear mother rest.

Look good[4] an' find it, Willie dear,
    See dat from bush 'tis free;
Remember that my heart is near,
    An' you say you lub me.

An' plant on it my fav'rite fern,
    Which I be'n usual wear;
In days to come I shall return
    To end my wand'rin's dere.

---

4. Carefully.

To Bennie

(In Answer to a Letter)

You say, dearest comrade, my love has grown
    cold,
But you are mistaken, it burns as of old;
And no power below, dearest lad, nor above,
Can ever lessen, frien' Bennie, my love.

Could you but look in my eyes, you would see
That 'tis a wrong thought you have about me;
Could you but feel my hand laid on your head,
Never again would you say what you've said.

Naught, o my Bennie, our friendship can sever,
Dearly I love you, shall love you for ever;
Moment by moment my thoughts are of you,
Trust me, oh, trust me, for aye to be true.

Hopping off the Tram

It would not stop,
So I took a hop,
An', Lard oh, my foot a miss![1]
It sent me do'n
Slam on de groun',
An' I had a dusty kiss.

The car went 'long
With its hummin' song,
An' I too went my way;
But the sudden fall
I did recall,
And shall for many a day.

---

1. Tripped.

To a Comrade[1]

Little comrade, never min'
Though another is unkin';
"Of de pain o' dis ya wul'
We must suck we bellyful."[2]

Little comrade, moan not so,
Oh, you fill my heart with woe!
Sad I listen to your cries,
Can't you ope your burnin' eyes?

Little comrade, though 'tis hot,[3]
Say you will revenge him not:[4]
Talk not thus, you mek me grieve,
Promise me you will forgive.

Little comrade, never min'
Though a brother is unkin';
Treat him kindest as you can,
Show yourself the better man.

---

1. A corrosive fluid had been wilfully thrown in his face.—*Au.*
2. See "*Whe' fe do*, which the author and his little comrade had been reading together.
3. Painful.
4. Tell me you will not take vengeance on him.

JUBBA[1]

My Jubba waiting dere fe me;
Me, knowin', went out on de spree,
An' she, she wait deh till midnight,
Bleach-bleachin' in de cold moonlight:
An' when at last I did go home
I found out dat she had just come,
An' now she tu'n her back away,
An' won't listen a wud I say.

    Forgive me, Jubba, Jubba dear,
    As you are standing, standing there,
    An' I will no more mek you grieve,
    My Jubba, ef you'll but forgive.

I'll go to no more dancing booth,
I'll play no more wid flirty Ruth,
I didn' mean a t'ing, Jubba,
I didn' know you'd bex fe da';
I only took two set o' dance
An' at de bidding[2] tried me chance;
I buy de big crown-bread fe you,
An' won't you tek it, Jubba?—do.

    Forgive me, Jubba, Jubba dear, etc.

It was a nice tea-meeting though,
None o' de boy dem wasn' slow,
An' it was pack' wid pretty gal,
So de young man was in dem sall;[3]
But when I 'member you a yard[4]
I know dat you would t'ink it hard,

---

1. The *u* has the value of the *oo* in *look*.
2. An auction of loaves of fine bread, profusely decorated by the baker's art, is a feature of rustic dances.
3. So the young men had a fine time of it.
4. In the yard, *i.e.*, at home.

Aldough, Jubba, 'twas sake o' spite
Mek say you wouldn' come te-night.[5]

    Forgive me, Jubba, Jubba dear, etc.

I lef' you, Jub, in such a state,
I neber knew dat you would wait i
Yet all de while I couldn' res',
De t'ought o' you was in me breas';
So nummo time I couldn' was'e,
But me go get me pillow-case[6]
An' put in deh you bread an' cake
Forgive me, Jubba, fe God sake!

    Forgive me, Jubba, Jubba dear, etc.

---

5. Out of caprice Jubba had refused to go to the dance: she was jealously watching outside the booth, while her young man imagined she was at home.
6. The usual receptacle for bread.

Taken Aback

Let me go, Joe, for I want go home: Can't

stan' wid you, For pa might go come;

An' if him on-ly hab him rum, I

don't know what-e-ber I'll do.

Go wid you, Joe?—you don't lub me den! I

shame o' you—Gals caan' trust you men! An

I be'n tek-in' you fe me frien'; Good-

night, Joe, you've prov-en un-true.

PLEADING

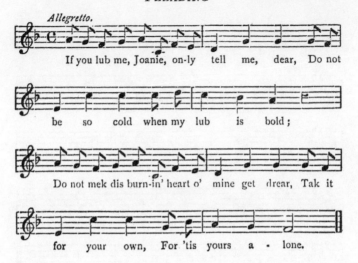

Allegretto.

If you lub me, Joanie, on-ly tell me, dear, Do not be so cold when my lub is bold; Do not mek dis burn-in' heart o' mine get drear, Tak it for your own, For 'tis yours a - lone.

IONE

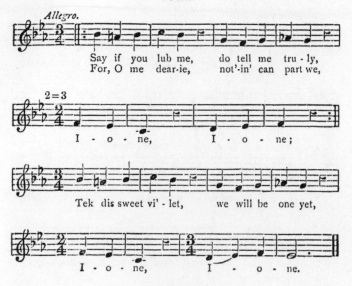

Allegro.

Say if you lub me, do tell me tru - ly,
For, O me dear-ie, not'-in' can part we,

2 = 3

I - o - ne, I - o - ne;

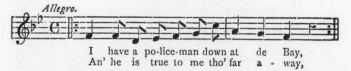

Tek dis sweet vi' - let, we will be one yet,

I - o - ne, I - o - ne.

MY PRETTY DAN

Allegro.

I have a po-lice-man down at de Bay,
An' he is true to me tho' far a - way,

alla fine.

far a - way.

My Soldier Lad

See yonder soldier lad in zouave jac-ket clad? His lov-in' heart is mine, His heart so bright an' glad; My soul an' spirit com-bine to love my sol-dier lad. O my dear lil-ly sol-dier lad, I am true an' so are you, And oh, my lov-in' heart is glad— For I know that you are true.

JUBBA.

My Jub-ba wait-ing dere fe
me; Me, knowin', went out on de spree, An' she, she
wait deh till mid-night, Bleach-bleachin' in de cold moon-
light: An' when at last I did go home I found out
dat she had just come, An' now she tu'n her back a-
way, An' won't list-en a wud I say. Forgive me
Jub-ba, Jub-ba dear, As you are stand-in', stand-in'

there, An' I will no more mek you grieve, My Jub-ba,

ef you'll but for - give ———, An' I will no more mek you

grieve, My Jub-ba ef you'll but for - give.

A Note About the Author

Claude McKay (1889–1948) was a Jamaican poet and novelist. Born in Sunny Ville, Jamaica, McKay was raised in a strict Baptist family alongside seven siblings. Sent to live with his brother Theo, a journalist, at the age of nine, McKay excelled in school while reading poetry in his free time. In 1912, he published his debut collection *Songs of Jamaica*, the first poems written in Jamaican Patois to appear in print. That same year, he moved to the United States to attend the Tuskegee Institute, though he eventually transferred to Kansas State University. Upon his arrival in the South, he was shocked by the racism and segregation experienced by Black Americans, which—combined with his reading of W. E. B. Du Bois' work—inspired him to write political poems and to explore the principles of socialism. He moved to New York in 1914 without completing his degree, turning his efforts to publishing poems in *The Seven Arts* and later *The Liberator*, where he would serve as co-executive editor from 1919 to 1922. Over the next decade, he would devote himself to communism and black radicalism, joining the Industrial Workers of the World, opposing the efforts of Marcus Garvey and the NAACP, and travelling to Britain and Russia to meet with communists and write articles for various leftist publications. McKay, a bisexual man, was also a major figure of the Harlem Renaissance, penning *Harlem Shadows* (1922), a successful collection of poems, and *Home to Harlem* (1928), an award-winning novel exploring Harlem's legendary nightlife.

A Note from the Publisher

Spanning many genres, from non-fiction essays to literature classics to children's books and lyric poetry, Mint Edition books showcase the master works of our time in a modern new package. The text is freshly typeset, is clean and easy to read, and features a new note about the author in each volume. Many books also include exclusive new introductory material. Every book boasts a striking new cover, which makes it as appropriate for collecting as it is for gift giving. Mint Edition books are only printed when a reader orders them, so natural resources are not wasted. We're proud that our books are never manufactured in excess and exist only in the exact quantity they need to be read and enjoyed.

bookfinity™

Discover more of your favorite classics with Bookfinity™.

- Track your reading with custom book lists.
- Get great book recommendations for your personalized Reader Type.
- Add reviews for your favorite books.
- AND MUCH MORE!

Visit **bookfinity.com** and take the fun Reader Type quiz to get started.

Enjoy our classic and modern companion pairings!

Classic & Modern